The System of Things III

I Took a Stand

FOR

JOHN BUMPAS JR + FAMILY

OS-11-21

Luis E. Sweeney

Fulton Books, Inc.
Meadville, PA

Published by Fulton Books 2020

ISBN 978-1-64952-197-2 (paperback)
ISBN 978-1-64952-198-9 (digital)

Printed in the United States of America

I would like to dedicate this book to everyone who lives and who have died taking a stand against racism and the injustice that has and is taking place within our government, society, and the world today. Fore, that task is a heavy burden. If one really thinks about it, whether one believes in the *Lord* or not, a reality and fact is this: one lives and one dies.

I truly believe before one's eyes closes for the last time, the mystery will be known whether there is and/or isn't a *God* in heaven. I pray while one is yet aboveground to take in consideration and have an open mind and believe there is a reason for everything and nothing happens by chance. Take heed of the vision of John D. Robinson.

Sincerely yours and thank you,
Luis E. Sweeney

CONTENTS

PROLOGUE

It had been a very busy day and night. The party poppers, balloons, and all the other paraphernalia that was usually associated with an event and/or party were the only remnants that were left within the majority of the campaign headquarters.

The celebrations and the I-wish-you-the-best complements had already been said and done. The city, county, and state elections were finally over. The citizens on August 5, 2010, had cast their votes.

As fate would have it, on August 6, 2010, at about 1:30 a.m., in the morning, John was in his bed thinking about the results of the sheriff's race.

He was lying down and was staring at the ceiling fan when he said, "I'll be damned. Those low-down dirty rotten scoundrels had done it again."

After realizing what he said was out loud, he quietly leaned over his wife's shoulder to look and see if he had awakened her. It had been a long day and night for her as well, especially after seeing what he had gone through during the sheriff's race.

John knew she would have been worried about him and would have wondered why he was still awake.

His daughter was also asleep in her bedroom. It had been a long day and night for her as well. She had been coming home periodically during the sheriff's race to be with her parents.

At the time, she was a junior in college. It was located in another county. Her major was in prelaw. Her plans were to go to a law school in Atlanta, Georgia. John was anticipating on utilizing her services upon her graduation.

Having that being said, and without saying another word out loud, he tried to be as quiet as a mouse.

Actually, the only noise that could be heard in his house other than him moving around was the sound of the air and heating system kicking on and off and the whooshing sound of the air circulating within the ventilation system.

John clamped his fingers together behind his head as he stared at the ceiling fan again. He was thinking about what his next strategic move was going to be. He was upset, disappointed, and proud at the same time.

A precedent had been set, and history was once again being made that involved him. He was thinking about that. As a result, he had a hard time trying to go to sleep.

I should have known they would do something like that to stop me, John quietly said to himself.

Unlike the previous events and treacherous acts that they had done in the past, what they had recently done was considered to have been their masterpiece. They had managed for the second time to change the rules, regulations, policies, procedures, and the law.

Having that being said, with a determined look and smile upon his face, John proudly and quietly said, "I must have been the most feared man in the county for them to have gone to the extreme to do what they had done. They hadn't heard the last from me. The sheriff's race, as far as I am concerned, isn't over with yet!"

BOOK ONE

Those Low-Down Dirty Rotten Scoundrels

Having that being said, John *imagined* seeing all those scoundrels and collaborators sitting together in the sheriff's crowded campaign headquarters.

The room was filled with smoke that was emitting from their fat expensive cigars. They all were conversing, laughing, and drinking their alcoholic beverages that were concealed in plastic and foam cups. They were giving themselves the high five and the thumbs-up sign. They were celebrating the victory of the sheriff being reelected.

John *imagined* seeing Charlie with a smile on his face. He was bragging and saying to the others in the room, *We fixed him! Who does he think he is? He must have forgotten who I am. I run this town. He should have known that a long time ago. He knew the governor and the commissioner of the highway patrol were my friends.*

John *imagined* the sheriff responding by saying, *You're right, Charlie! We wouldn't have been able to control the boy. I know for a fact that he wouldn't have gone along with what we would have wanted him to do for us. It's a shame! I really like the boy. He has guts! He is different from the rest of them.*

John *imagined* seeing the rest of the good old boys. They all were laughing when someone said, *You're right, Sheriff! That boy is just like a fly on the wall. Somehow, he seems to hear and see everything we do. He's like a busy bee. If we swat at him and miss, he would sting the heck out of us.*

Having that being said, according to the gossip John had heard and what he was told when he first arrived in the county, Charlie was a businessman, who had made a fortune in the medical supply business.

He, in John's opinion, had similar characteristics as Boss Hogg, the character that was seen on the television show called *The Dukes of Hazzard.*

It had been rumored that Charlie was the sheriff's financial backer, and the sheriff had appointed him to a position within his department. Charlie was appointed to being the supervisor over the Sheriff's Deputy Reserve Unit.

It was also said that the sheriff allowed Charlie to have police emergency equipment installed in his personal vehicle.

As far as John was concerned, the old saying "I'll scratch your back if you scratch my back" was true. It was the good old boy system of things.

Having that being said, in spite of what was done to John, he really had no hard feelings toward Charlie or the sheriff. He liked them both even though he suspected them of being the ringleaders involved in what was done to him. He just couldn't prove it.

John knew how the game was played. He knew from the very beginning how important the 2010 sheriff's race meant to them.

It just so happened the sheriff's twenty-year pension was on the line. The sheriff had to win in order to get his pension in 2014, which could have been just a coincident, and then again, it could have been the very reason behind what was done to John and why.

As for the other scoundrels, John was referring to the individuals who at one time worked for the government as well as those who at the time currently worked for the government, specifically within the highway patrol division, the Sheriff Department, the Equal Employment Opportunity Division, and those good old boys within the county of which he resided.

As fate would have it, at the time, John was a twenty-two-year veteran of the highway patrol. He was a state trooper, and he only had three years to go before he was going to retire.

It just so happened there was a mandatory policy for a trooper below the rank of a sergeant to retire at the age of sixty.

He had been thinking about his future beyond the highway patrol uniform. He decided to be a candidate in the 2010 sheriff's race.

Having that being said, it just so happened the current sheriff and a local city fireman named Terry were the other candidates vying for that position.

Terry was also a local county magistrate. His position as a local fireman and a county magistrate was another example of the good old boy system of things in the county.

John thought about what Terry had said in one of his campaign speeches. He said, "The sheriff and I are good friends. I had worked as a member of his Drug Task Force. I live in the same section of town where the sheriff lives. I plan to run a clean campaign."

As far as John was concerned, they were still good buddies. He knew they had hoped he wouldn't have gotten involved in the sheriff's race as a candidate.

John then thought about what the sheriff had said in one of his campaign speeches. The sheriff said, "I plan to run my campaign as clean as possible as long as the others do the same."

After John heard that, he quietly said, *Yeah! Right!* John knew the sheriff had the advantage as being the incumbent.

John believed the majority of those scoundrels might have thought of him as being a renegade, a troublemaker, a nonconformists, and, of all things, a whistleblower.

He believed those were probably the nicest thoughts they had of him. He could only imagine the names that they really called him while they were behind closed doors and among themselves, especially after he had written two books titled *The System of Things I* and *The System of Things II: True Justice Went to Hell.*

Those books were written as a result of the injustice that he had seen taking place within the government, specifically corruption, retaliation, and racism of which he was a victim thereof.

Having that being said, it wasn't John's intent initially to upset them by writing those books. He just wanted to get their attention. He had already talked to his immediate superiors before he had written those books. He wanted them to know how he felt and how he was being treated.

They all ignored him. They acted as if he didn't know what he was talking about and that they were his friends. It just so happened he had gotten his so-called friends' attention in a way that they didn't expect and/or like.

John didn't play their game the way that they had expected him to. He believed they were expecting him to be their yes man with a badge.

He wasn't afraid to say what was on his mind, and that, in his opinion, was probably one of the other things they didn't like about him. He didn't bow down to the good old boys or to anyone else for that matter.

John had sworn an oath to protect and serve the citizens of the county in which he resided as well as anyone else that would have come across his path. He was one of those individuals who had taken an oath seriously. He believed in the integrity of the badge that he wore on his uniform.

Having that being said, John *imagined* seeing the evil ones walking back and forth and scratching their heads. They were trying to figure out how in the world he had managed to still be employed.

John *imagined* them saying, *After all of the things we had done to him, he's still here. He has the nerve and the courage to stand up to us. What is wrong with him? He is differently not like the others. We've got to find a way to be rid of him. He might stir up the rest of them.*

It just so happened John was aware for quite some time that they had been plotting against him. He knew they had hoped if enough pressure was put on him, he would quit.

John apparently had become a thorn in their side, a rock in their shoe, and/or perhaps their medicine, specifically "castor oil."

John *imagined* hearing someone say, *Something is wrong here! He is supposed to be uncomfortable around us. He sure doesn't act like it.*

Having that being said, John thought about the times when he had approached them. Some of them appeared to have been apprehensive and were very cautious of what they would say and/or do in his presence.

He had often heard them whispering and say, "Hey! Here he comes!"

John believed they must have thought that he wasn't aware of what they would say. In fact, when he heard them saying things like that, it made him feel proud of knowing that they were afraid to say and/or do anything in front of him that would have been deemed inappropriate.

On the other hand, it made him feel sad, and on occasions, tears would form in his eyes when he thought about it. He never thought someone would feel uncomfortable around him.

Having that being said, as he remembered thinking about it, tears began to form in his eyes. He began to wonder what in the world did he do and/or have said to become such a threat to them. He knew he hadn't said anything about them that weren't true, and he hadn't done anything to them that wasn't deserved.

As fate would have it, John didn't believe in coincidences. He believed there was a reason for everything and nothing happen by chance.

Book Two

John's Vision

As John continued thinking about the events that had taken place during the sheriff's race, he thought about the time when he had first arrived in the county. He didn't know anyone or anything about the county.

As fate would have it, it didn't take him long to find out that the county he was assigned to was well-known as being a racist county. He was told that a slave was hung at the county courthouse square.

He was told that the citizens celebrated an event known as the Mule Day Celebration while mules were sold during that celebration, and in the past, the selling of slaves was the main attraction.

John found out that the county in which he resided was next to Giles County, and Giles County was well-known as being the home of a racist organization called Ku Klux Klan.

He also found out that the county in which he resided was famously known as a result of the race riots that had taken place there in 1947.

Having that being said, and the more John thought about it, he began to believe the department's reason for assigning him to the county in the first place was motivated beyond what he originally thought.

He at first thought it was because there was a vacant position in the district and in the county that needed to be filled.

As fate would have it, his reasoning and thoughts had begun to change. He believed there were three other possible reasons, and one was because of his faith in the Lord, *Jesus Christ*. He believed his faith was being tested, and two, he began to believe it was the result of a conspiracy by certain individuals within the department to have a reason to terminate him and, three, to indirectly cause him physical harm and/or to get him to quit because of the known fact that he was the only Black trooper in the entire district.

Having that being said, and while thinking about that, he finally drifted off to sleep.

As fate would have it, as he slept, he had a dream and a vision. He *imagined* hearing the Lord say to several angels, *You'll be very busy with this one. He is going to be tested and persecuted for my namesake.*

What did the Lord mean by that? John remembered saying to himself in his vision.

He was wondering who it was that the Lord was referring to when, all of a sudden and somehow, he realized that the Lord was talking about him, and in that instant, John began to see the reflection of his life through his memory of it.

He was able to remember as far back as to when he was five years old, and it seemed like to him that he was watching a movie of his own life. He saw himself living in Fort Richardson, Alaska. He remembered when he said, "Mom, who is God?"

John didn't know why he had asked his mother that. In fact, it was amazing to him to know and realized that was the very first thing that he could remember in his past.

The question totally caught his mother off guard. She turned around to look at him. She wondered what would make him asked that. She'd never before had a deep discussion with him about who God was.

She gained her composure, and then she went to get a King James Version of the Bible. She then sat John upon her lap.

As John remembered, he saw himself patiently waiting for his mother to start reading to him. He stared into her eyes. He saw a strange look upon his mother's face when she noticed that he was staring at her eyes. It was as if his curious baby brown eyes had put her in a trance. She began to read to him.

Having that being said, John didn't remember how far she had read and/or what she had actually read. It was apparently enough to satisfy him. He saw himself jumping off her lap and going outside to play.

John remembered a story that his mother had once told him about when he was a baby. She said to him, "One day, you were in your stroller when I heard a loud noise of the stroller going down the basement stairs.

"The stairs were a long way down to the basement floor. The basement was a fallout shelter. It was dug very deep into the ground.

"I didn't know what to expect. I ran down the basement stairs, and I noticed that your feet were positioned as if something was holding them up. Your feet apparently had not touched the steps when you took that long ride down the basement stairs. You were laughing as if it was fun. The Lord must have been with you. You must have had a guardian angel watching over you."

John believed it was meant for him to have been born and raised within a military environment. He was taught to love God, his family, and his country.

While in school, he was taught to understand the importance of discipline and following rules, regulations, policies, and procedures.

He was exposed to the military way of life and doing things. He was taught to never give up, and it was always emphasized that he could be whatever he wanted to be and to not let anyone stop him from obtaining his dream.

He believed the best benefit of being a child raised up within a military environment was having friends of all colors and being able to travel throughout the United States and other countries.

As John saw himself growing older, he could tell there was something different about him in comparison to his peers.

He participated in the normal childhood games and sports, and he noticed that he was very good at whatever he participated in.

He began to notice that he felt compassion toward other people who he thought were less fortunate than he was, and at times, he wondered why he felt that way.

John remembered seeing certain events taking place in his life that made him aware of how important life really was. He believed it was at that time that it was meant for him to begin to recognize the Lord's presence in his life.

As fate would have it, John's father had a part-time job working at a military golf club. It was his way of playing golf for free and earning extra income at the same time.

It just so happened one nice sunny evening, Sonny, John's older brother, and he were riding in a golf cart with their father when it ran out of gas. They weren't too far from the lodge when that happened. Their father said, "I want you two to stay in the golf cart and to wait for me to bring back some gasoline."

It just so happened daylight didn't last that long during a certain season in Alaska. It was that season.

While Sonny and John were waiting for their father to return, it started to get dark. It made John nervous.

The problem that John had was the fact that there were about twenty moose not too far from where they were. The moose were eating grass, and John was afraid. He had seen moose attack people before, especially when their calves were around, and it just so happened their calves were around them eating grass too.

John remembered saying to Sonny, "Sonny, when is dad coming back?"

"I don't know," Sonny responded.

"Let's go to the lodge," John suggested.

Sonny agreed with John. They got out of the golf cart and proceeded toward the lodge.

Sonny walked toward the lodge as if nothing was wrong. He never did turn around to look at the moose. John did. In fact, he kept on looking back at the moose as he was walking away from them.

Having that being said, it was a wonder that John didn't trip over something and had fallen.

As fate would have it, it was a good thing that John was looking. He screamed and said, "Sonny! The moose are coming after us!"

Sonny turned around. His eyes seemed to have been as big as a golf ball. He said to John, "Run! Run as fast as you can!"

John was running as fast as he could. He was running before he had called out to Sonny.

He could hear the moose running as if there was a stampede. He felt the ground shaking below his feet. He was terrified.

There could have been more, but all he knew at that time was there was one big moose breathing down on his neck. John felt its hot breath.

John turned around to see, and all that he could see was the moose's face and its big eyes beaming down at him. He believed the moose's face was bigger than his whole body. He screamed.

As fate would have it, as soon as the moose was about to get John, his father came out of the lodge, and when the door shut, it made a loud noise. It sounded as if a gun had been fired, and as far as John knew, it could have been gunfire. His father was known to carry a weapon.

The moose stopped in their tracks, and they all ran away. It was just in the nick of time.

Having that been said, John remembered as soon as he regained his composure, a strange sensation came upon him. It was something that he hadn't remembered ever feeling before at that time.

Somehow, he knew the Lord was involved. He felt that his brother and he had been protected.

As time passed, John had turned ten years old. Hon. John F. Kennedy was the president of the United States.

John remembered some of the events that had taken place during Kennedy's presidency, specifically his famous speech when he said, "Ask not what your country can do for you. Ask what you can do for your country." John also remembered the Cuban Missile Crisis.

At the time, Fort Richardson was an army missile base. The air alert siren had activated. It was an alarm that no one actually expected would be activated.

John heard it. It caught his family and him by surprise. He heard airplanes and helicopters hovering in the sky and the military police saying on their loudspeakers, "Everyone go to your basements! Go to your basements immediately! It's not a drill!"

The ground began to shake, and it wasn't the result of an earthquake.

John believed the missiles were being prepped to be activated, and there was nothing that he or his family could do but to wait and to see what was going to happen next.

His father made sure that they were all right before he rushed out of the house. He headed toward the mountain. That was where his base was.

John's family and he had huddled together in the basement. They all were quiet. He helped himself to several cans of C rations.

C rations were condensed food that was in metal cans. C rations were available in the case of emergencies and were kept in the basement where the temperature was always cool.

It was an emergency as far as John was concerned. He had always wanted to know what peanut butter would taste like on those big white soda crackers.

As he sat there munching on those soda crackers, he thought about the military war movies that he had seen that pertained to people in other countries having to go to their fallout shelters as a result of an air raid. He had always wondered how those people must have felt.

As fate would have it, it had come to pass. John knew how it felt, and as a result, he thought about the Lord again.

It didn't take that long before he heard the military police saying on their loudspeakers, "The crisis is over! The crisis is over! You can come out of your basements!"

John knew enough to know that Alaska would have been Russia's first target.

Having that being said, it seemed like to John that he was getting a dose of crisis, one after another.

It just so happened as time passed, there was an earthquake in 1964, and to John's knowledge, it was the worst recorded earthquake Alaska has ever had. It occurred on Good Friday.

As fate would have it, the strange thing about that earthquake was the fact that there were two other minor earthquakes prior to that one that also took place on Good Friday.

That really got John's attention, and those facts really got him to thinking about the Lord.

After the earthquake had taken place, John's father received new military orders. He was ordered to go to Maine.

He heard his father say, "Lois, there isn't an army military base in Maine. There is only an air force base there. The military had apparently made a mistake in my military orders."

Lois was John's mother's name. His father planned on taking advantage of that mistake. He didn't question his military orders. He was going to report to where he was told. He was going to consider it as being a vacation.

John remembered when he helped loading up the Pontiac. He thought traveling by car wasn't going to be so bad. His attitude had changed when they reached the Alcan Highway.

The Alcan Highway was the way out at the time. It was a long deserted stretch of highway made mostly of dirt and rocks, and there were only a few guardrails visible as far as John could see and remember.

At times, John's family would be the only people on the highway. That really made him nervous. His attitude had gotten worse.

He became concerned about the possibility of the car breaking down. He also thought about the different types of animals that would love to have had his family and him over for dinner.

John prayed and said, "Lord, please protect my family and me during this long trip. Help us be safe." He believed that was the first time that he thought there was a need for him to really pray.

He tried very hard to go to sleep. He thought by sleeping he would miss out on all the possible dangers that could take place throughout the trip. He thought by the time he would have awakened, they would have been off the highway and the mountain that they were on. He knew the only way they were going to survive the journey was with the help of the Lord.

Having that being said, he finally went to sleep, and as time passed, which he thought wasn't long enough, he heard his mother say, "John! Wake up! Wake up! I want you to see this!"

John's mother appeared to have been very excited as she was shaking him. His eyes were barely opened when he looked out of the window. He didn't know they were at the very top of the mountain. He didn't see the edge of the road when he looked out of the window. He screamed. The only thing he did see was down a valley. He thought he was going to have a heart attack. It almost scared him to death. He thought the car had veered off the road.

It took him a while to regain his composure, and after thinking about it, he said, "Mom, it was a once-in-a-lifetime view to see. I'm glad you had awakened me."

John remembered as time passed, it started to get dark, and it began to snow. He saw a few signs indicating that the Canadian border wasn't that far away from where they were.

As fate would have it, it began to snow very fast. It had gotten to the point where the snow blinded everyone. They could hardly see anything outside the car. Some people called it whiteout.

John's father had gotten out of the car. He walked in front of the car while Lois drove. That was the only way they could make it.

Having that being said, and as time passed, it stopped snowing after John's father had walked about two miles. It didn't take long to reach the Canadian border after that.

His father's military orders were checked, and he was given permission to continue on through Canada.

It just so happened his father drove to a town called Whitehorse. He was looking for a hotel. He saw a sign that stated that there were rooms available for rent. John was glad. He was tired and ready to go to sleep again.

As fate would have it, his father went in the hotel, and when he came back, he was mad.

"The clerk wouldn't let me rent a room because of the color of my skin," John's father said to Lois.

That was the first time in John's life that he realized the color of one's skin really made a difference in how one would be treated.

As fate would have it, his father was able to rent a room at another hotel.

John remembered that night. That night wasn't a good night for him. He thought about what had happened to his father.

I hate all White people, John said to himself as he drifted off to sleep.

Having that being said, the following day, they continued on their journey. John was still thinking about what had happened to his father when all of a sudden the car engine malfunctioned, and as fate would have it, they weren't too far from a service station.

John was glad that at least they weren't on that mountain and on the Alcan Highway. *That was a blessing in itself*, he thought.

His father had the car towed to the closest service station. John and Sonny went with their father to the service station. John's mother and his little brothers and sisters went to a restaurant to eat.

It just so happened the owner of the service station was going to charge John's father a lot of money to fix the car engine. His father knew there was nothing that he could do about it. He was at the mercy of the owner of the service station.

As fate would have it, John saw a White man, who worked there, slip his father a note saying, "Sir, I'm sorry you are being treated this way. The price he is charging you is not right. Have your car towed to this address and give this note to this person. He'll fix your car at a reasonable price. I hate to see someone being taken advantage of."

John then saw a smile come upon his father's face, and as a result, he smiled too. He then realized that he couldn't hate a whole race of people because of the action of another person. He believed it was the Lord's will for him to have witnessed that transaction.

As he thought about it, he believed it was at that time in his life that the Lord wanted him to feel the effect of racism and the evil it represented.

He made a covenant with the Lord. He said, "Lord, I will never treat a human being differently because of the color of one's skin, and I won't let anyone treat me differently because of the color of my skin. I will always take a stand against racism."

As fate would have it, and as time passed, they finally reached their destination.

It just so happened, while in Maine, John didn't remember seeing any other Black families. However, he did see several Indians, and he had an opportunity to go to a real Indian traders post. That was very educational for him.

Having that being said and as time passed, he remembered one boring day he was sitting outside in his yard. His neighbor had a family get-together. There were adults and kids playing croquet. They were having a good time.

He was sitting down in the grass with his hands under his chin. He was watching them playing croquet. They must have thought about him as he was watching them. They invited him to their family gathering.

"Do you want to play croquet?" someone had asked John.

"I don't know how," he responded.

"I'll teach you how to play," the person said.

John actually had fun. They made him feel welcomed, and they all were White.

Having that being said and as time passed, the Military had corrected their error. His father was given new military orders. He was assigned to Fort Knox, Kentucky.

His father's so-called vacation was over. They loaded up the Pontiac and were once again heading toward another destination.

Having that being said, while they were in route to Kentucky, John's family had the opportunity to travel through the majority of the thirteen colonies. He was also able to go to the New York World's Fair in 1964.

As time passed, they finally reached their new destination. They made it!

John remembered the good times and experiences that he had while living in Alaska. He really didn't want to leave. He loved being there.

Having that being said, it took him a while to get used to living in Fort Knox.

As time passed, he saw himself participating in several sports in and out of school. He became an all-star player in every sport that he participated in.

As fate would have it, one day, he had to play a game on the school basketball team. It was a big game for him. That game was going to be his last one. His father had received orders to go to Vietnam.

The principal made an announcement on the loudspeaker and said, "This will be the last game that John, our star player, will be playing. His father has been ordered to go to Vietnam. John will be leaving us.

"I want to take this time to say that we appreciate the hard work he has done and the time he has been with us. We wish him and his family the very best."

John remembered he was standing in the middle of the basketball court at that time. Tears had form in his eyes. Everyone had given him a standing ovation.

As John thought about that, he felt the saddest part about being a military child was the fact that he had to move constantly and away from the friends that he had made.

Having that being said and as fate would have it, John's mother and father were born and raised in Nashville. Most of their family and friends lived there. As a result, John's father and mother decided to move the family to Nashville.

Book Three

Cultural Shock

John remembered when he moved to east Nashville. East Nashville was considered to be the most popular middle-class Black neighborhood at the time.

It was the first time that John had to live among so many people of his same race at one time and in one place. It was a *culture shock* for him.

He went to Isaac Litton Junior High School. It was predominately a White-populated school. He noticed that the Black kids associated more with each other, and the White kids associated more with each other.

He found himself to be in a unique position. He associated with the Black and White kids, and it was very noticeable throughout the school.

As a result, he became well-liked by the staff and the majority of all the students instantly. As far as he was concerned, everything was going just fine until Rev. Martin Luther King Jr. was assassinated.

The assassination reminded him of the assassination of President John F. Kennedy. John was ten years old at that time.

Having that being said, John didn't know anything about Rev. Martin Luther King Jr. He didn't understand why Black and White people were fighting each other. He didn't realize there was so much hatred between the two races until he had seen what was taking place on television.

He saw White police officers and White national guardsmen beating up Black men, women, and children and commanding their dogs to attack them. He saw racial slurs and writings on walls, banners, and other things.

As a result, it affected him. He then remembered the incidence that took place in Canada and the covenant he had made with the Lord.

As fate would have it, it was then that he thought about becoming a law enforcement officer. He wanted to be in a position of power and to have authority. He wanted it to be known that whoever would come in contact with him would know that they would be treated fair and justly. He wanted it to be known that the color of one's skin wouldn't affect his judgment in the way that he would enforce the law.

Having that being said, the problem that he had was the fact that he wasn't old enough to become a policeman.

As time passed and after things had calmed down, John began to enjoy his position and status in the neighborhood as well as in school, and according to his Black and White friends, he was different.

John's accent was different from theirs, and they enjoyed listening to him talk about what he had done, where he had been, and what he had seen.

Having that being said and as time passed, John began to catch onto the slang words that his friends would say, and as fate would have it, his father returned home safely. He retired shortly afterward.

As time passed, in 1970, Sonny and several of his friends decided to join the Army during the Vietnam War. They knew there was a good chance of them being drafted, and if they were drafted, the Military would assign them to any position or field that they wanted them to be in. They took a chance and joined.

As fate would have it, Sonny was fortunate. He didn't have to go to Vietnam. His friends weren't so lucky. John believed that was another indicator and a sign for him to know that the Lord was continuously protecting him and his family.

In the meantime, John saw himself becoming accustomed to civilian life. He began to hang out in the streets with his friends.

It was something that he hadn't done before. He began to get in trouble.

One day, Thomas drove his car in front of John's house, and John noticed that there was a White guy sitting in the front passenger seat.

Thomas was John's best friend, and he lived across the street from him.

"Hey, man! How about riding with us?" Thomas said.

John was bored, and he said, "Okay."

John sat in the back seat of the car behind the front passenger's seat, and he noticed they had a can of beer in their hand. Thomas asked John if he wanted one. John said, "Sure."

It just so happened and to John's surprise, Thomas drove behind their school, and he parked in the parking lot near the gymnasium. It was about 10:00 p.m.

"There are some drums that were left in the gymnasium after the talent show. We are going to steal them," they both said to John.

"I'm not stealing any drums," John said.

"Okay! Just stay here then," they said.

Having that being said, John felt uncomfortable sitting in the car all by himself. He thought about getting out of the car and to walk home.

However, he decided not to because he was too far from home, and he didn't feel like walking. So he stayed in the car while they broke into the gymnasium.

As he sat in the car, he began to think about what he would do and say if the police came to the car and would asked him what he was doing sitting in the car all by himself at that time of night and behind the school gymnasium. He knew he wouldn't have had a good answer and/or a reason. Thomas and the White guy had put him in a heck of a spot.

He then decided to go down to the school where they were to keep from being put in that situation. They stole the drums and had placed them in the car. John helped them put the drums in the car since he was there.

While in the car, Thomas and the White guy discussed where they were going to take the drums. John didn't say a word. He was nervous, and he felt guilty.

Thomas drove John home first, and he asked John if they could keep the drums over his house until the morning. He hesitantly agreed.

Having that being said, when he went to school the next day, he heard people talking about the break in and the theft of the drums. He heard someone say, "Somebody broke in the school gym last night and had stolen the drums that were left there. Whoever had done it had gotten away with it clean." John felt relieved after hearing that.

As fate would have it, several weeks after the theft of the drums had taken place, an unmarked police car pulled up in front of John's home. He knew he was in trouble especially after seeing Thomas and the White guy handcuffed and sitting in the back seat.

So much for getting away with it, John said to himself as a female police officer came to his front door.

She said, "Is John Robinson home?"

In a way, John wished he wasn't. He wanted to say, "No! He isn't!" He then said, "I'm John."

"Is it going to be necessary for me to place handcuffs on you?" the officer said.

"No," John said in a low tone of voice.

Man, I'm in trouble, John thought to himself.

She let him sit in the front seat of her patrol car. She then drove them to their school. She took them to the Principal's Office.

John was embarrassed. The only good thing going for him was the fact that he didn't have handcuffs on him. He had hoped that the perception of him not being handcuffed would seem like he wasn't in trouble.

The principal was shocked to see him.

"John, I can understand seeing those two but you," he said.

Having that being said, Thomas and the White guy told the principal that John wasn't aware of their plan to steal the drums. John felt relieved after they said that.

The officer then took them to the Metropolitan Juvenile Detention Center. They were placed in a holding cell. They had to stay there until their parents had come to get them.

"Man, what happen?" Thomas said to the White guy.

John thought Thomas was going to beat the guy up. The White guy kept the symbols after he had sold the drums, and it just so happened a friend of his came over to his house and had recognized the symbols that were there by a drum set. The symbols were his.

John couldn't believe how stupid that guy was. He wondered what made Thomas hooked up with that guy in the first place.

John's parents were the first ones to arrive. They brought Thomas's mother with them. Thomas and the White guy tried to help John out again by telling his parents that he didn't know what they were up to until it was too late. They were placed on probation for two weeks.

As fate would have it, two weeks later while in court, Thomas and the White guy testified, and they both said, "Your Honor, John didn't know what we were up to until it was too late."

"John, you might want to think again about whom you associate yourself with. You are fortunate that those two had spoken up for you. I am going to release you, and your record will be cleared. You will not be required to be on probation. But you two will be placed on probation, and you will have a juvenile record," the judge said.

The judge was referring to Thomas and the White guy.

As time passed, John tried to be a good boy, and Sonny had come home on a military leave. John was glad to see him. Sonny brought a nice car. John wished he had a car like the one Sonny brought.

He asked Sonny if he could take him to a football game. It was Friday night. Sonny took him to the football game.

As fate would have it, toward the end of the football game, John began to think about how he was going to get back home. He saw two friends of his named Joe and Berry. Joe lived up the street from him, and Berry lived in another area of the neighborhood.

John approached Berry and said, "Berry, how are you getting home?"

"I don't know," Berry said.

John saw Joe. Joe was quite a distance away from where Berry and him was. He also saw a cousin of his.

Having that being said, it looked like John's cousin, Joe, and a few other people were involved in a confrontation with someone.

John didn't know what was going on, and he really didn't care. He knew his cousin had a car. So he decided to ask his cousin for a ride home.

"Hey, cuz, can you give me a ride home?" John asked.

"Sure! Follow me," he said.

Joe, Berry, John, and another guy got in the car. The other guy's name was Gary.

John looked at Joe and said, "Joe, what happen to you?"

John could tell Joe had been in a fight. He looked scuffed up. Joe didn't say a word.

As fate would have it, John heard the sound of police sirens. His cousin was pulled over by several metro police officers. John wasn't worried about it because he hadn't done anything wrong.

"Get out of the car with your hands up," the police officers said.

They all got out of the car. John was embarrassed.

One officer asked them how old they were. Joe, Berry, and John were juveniles, and his cousin and Gary was eighteen years old.

The officers separated them by having Joe, Berry, and John to sit in the back seat of one police car, and John's cousin and Gary were placed in the back seat of another police car.

"We are taking those three to the Metropolitan Juvenile Detention Center and the others to jail," one officer said to another officer.

John heard one officer laugh and say, "We ought to take them all under the bridge before we do that."

Having that being said, all the officers were White, and John had heard of the police doing things like that before.

John remembered the first thing that came to his mind was the last time that he was taken to the detention center.

He said quietly, "Man! Not again!" Then he asked one officer, "Why am I being taken to the detention center?"

He was trying his best to get out of the predicament that he was in.

"We received a call that there was a fight in progress and that you all were involved," the office said.

"Look at me," John pleaded. "Does it look like I had been in a fight?" John said nervously.

"No, but he does," the officer said.

The officer was referring to Joe.

"Well, let me go. I wasn't involved," John said.

"I'm sorry. I can't," the officer replied.

John was in trouble again. He was with the wrong people at the wrong place and at the wrong time.

They arrived at the Metropolitan Juvenile Detention Center at about 11:30 p.m. There weren't any probation officers available. They were told that they had to stay the entire weekend.

Having that being said, when John was there before, he was able to see the rest of the inside of the detention center by looking at several monitors that were on the wall. He never thought he would wind up back there.

As for procedure, they had to take a shower before they were placed in an individual cell. John was the last one to take a shower, and he was the last one to be locked up in a cell.

He remembered entering the cell and hearing the sound of those keys jingling, the door opening, and the sound of the door slamming shut.

The sounds reminded him of the sounds he had heard when he watched those old prison movies while the prisoners wore black-and-white striped uniforms and had a ball and chain connected to their ankle.

He thought about his parents as a tear rolled down his face. He knew they were going to be disappointed in him again.

As fate would have it, the time was 12:01 a.m. John turned eighteen years old. It was his birthday. He turned eighteen years old locked up in a juvenile detention center.

He remembered saying, "Lord, there has got to be a reason for this to be happening to me. Here I am again locked up for something

I didn't do. Am I being punished for the things I had done and have gotten away with?"

After he said that, a strange sensation came upon him. He had felt that sensation before. He believed he felt the presence of the Lord with him.

He began to think about how blessed he was in spite of what was happening to him. He was innocent. He knew he didn't have to stay there no longer than two additional nights. He knew he could handle it, and most importantly, he realized if he had been eighteen years old, he would have been taken to jail. That alone had made him feel better.

He then suddenly realized there had to have been other people who were arrested and sent to jail and prisons for something that they hadn't done. He was a prime example.

As he thought about that, he believed that was what the Lord wanted him to know and to focus on instead of the fact of him being incarcerated.

It didn't take long before Monday had come. John survived the weekend. He was placed on probation until he had to appear in court.

As fate would have it, and as time passed, Joe, Berry, and John had appeared in court.

The victim said, "Your Honor, those two guys weren't involved. It was him!"

The victim was referring to Joe as being the one involved.

In that instant, tears began to form in John's eyes. He had a different perspective in how he felt about the criminal justice system and law enforcement. He realized that he was more interested in fairness and justice than the mere act of enforcing the law.

As he thought about that, he believed that was the Lord's intention as well.

As his vision continued, he remembered thinking about what he was going to do in life. He was very thankful and glad that his father was in the Military. His father was a drill sergeant. He always looked neat in his uniform.

John compared his father's uniform to that of a state trooper. It was mainly due to the fact that they both wore a similar hat. John thought it would be cool for him to become a state trooper someday.

Having that being said, he remembered talking to his uncle. His uncle was also named John. He was one of the first three Black state troopers to be hired in the state. He told John about some of his experiences.

He said he and the other two were treated very badly. They called him the N-word on many occasions to his face and when his back was turned. Someone had put sugar in the gas tank of his patrol car. They were given the worse assignments.

He said, very sadly, "John, if you ever become a trooper, don't owe them anything. They will hold that against you. They will think that they owned you. They will expect you to do everything they say."

As John thought about that, it reminded him of the time the department celebrated its seventy-fifth-year anniversary.

The department honored troopers and had displayed pictures of the history of the highway patrol on the walls at the main head-quarters and at the training academy.

Having that being said, the department didn't display a single picture of the first three Black state troopers that was hired.

John remembered how upset he was about that. He wrote a letter to the commissioner. He expressed how he felt. He wanted his uncle and the other two Black troopers to be honored as well.

As fate would have it, it came to pass. The commissioner had their picture placed in the seventy-fifth-year anniversary book but not on the walls at the headquarters and the training academy.

As time passed, John remembered graduating from high school. He wasn't old enough to become a state trooper. His parents wanted him to go to college. So he decided to apply to several universities.

He was accepted at Parson College in Iowa. His major was going to be in aviation. He thought he wanted to be a commercial airline pilot. His parents were so proud of him.

As fate would have it, John's girlfriend at the time said that she was pregnant. He thought about that. He was actually more concerned with his future child than he was with his girlfriend. He knew if by chance she decided not to be his girlfriend for whatever reason, he knew he could always get another girlfriend.

His plan had changed. He believed the Lord had something to do with it.

Book Four

The Military System of Things

John remembered when he decided to join the military, he knew it would have been hard for him to take care of his child and go to school at the same time. His decision didn't set well with his mother. His father understood.

Having that being said, the problem he had was deciding what branch of service to join. He thought about the Air Force since he was going to college to be a pilot.

His thoughts quickly changed. The Vietnam War was still going on, and there was still a possibility that he could be drafted. He thought about the possibility of the plane being shot down.

He then thought about the Navy and the probability of having to be around a lot of water. His thoughts quickly changed. He knew he couldn't outswim a shark if the ship was sunk.

He didn't consider the Marines at all. He knew they were the first ones to go to battle and the last ones to leave. He didn't want any part of that. So he decided to join the Army.

Having that being said and his mind made up, he didn't want to join by himself. He tried to talk Thomas into joining the Army with him. His plan didn't work. Thomas didn't want any part of it.

John remembered Thomas saying, "Man, are you crazy? You can count me out. It's no way that I'm going to join. There is a war going on you know. Have you forgotten about that? They would have to come and find me first."

Thomas and John laughed about it.

As fate would have it, John talked Ray into joining the Army with him. Ray was John's other best friend. The Army called it the buddy plan.

John remembered when Ray and he were preparing to be sworn in, John heard a voice say, "I'm sorry, sir. Could you please step out of the line?"

Ray was escorted out of the line. The Army wouldn't let him swear in because it was discovered that he had a criminal record. That left John by himself.

John was disappointed. He could tell that Ray really wanted to enlist. John felt sorry for him.

Having that being said, John remembered getting on the bus that was heading toward Fort Knox, Kentucky. The fact that he was really in the Army hadn't dawn on him.

Man, it's too late now. I'm stuck. Here I am heading toward Fort Knox as a soldier, and this time I'm not a child, he said quietly.

"Hey, Robinson! Hey, Robinson!" someone said out loud.

John turned around, and he saw another friend that he knew. His name was Charles.

Charles lived near John's neighborhood. They just so happened to be assigned to the same basic training camp, and then they were assigned to the same company barracks.

John felt a little better after knowing that. He believed the Lord had replaced one friend with another.

As time passed, Charles and John had completed basic training, and they were given their new duty assignments. It was the day that he was waiting on.

He was assigned to Fort Gordon, Georgia. That was where the Military Police Training School was being held. There was a big smile on his face. He was on his way to becoming a military policeman.

As fate would have it, and as time passed, John graduated from the Military Police School, and low and behold, President Nixon stopped sending soldiers to Vietnam. John's calculated risk had paid off.

Having that being said, he was then given another military order. He was ordered to attend a four-week Correctional Specialist School.

He didn't join the Army to work in a stockade, which was a military prison. He went to his sergeant and said, "Sergeant, I didn't sign up for this course."

"Soldier, all you have to do is to attend the first week. If you don't like it after that, go to the captain. He will take care of it for you," the sergeant said.

John could tell that the sergeant didn't appreciate him wanting to get out of attending that school.

In the meantime, John had contacted his recruiter. John said, "Going to that school wasn't a part of our agreement."

"There is nothing that I can do about that. The school will be beneficial to you," the recruiter said.

John was upset after hearing that. He also found out if he had failed any written test that he had taken during basic training, the Army could have assigned him to any position or field that they wanted him to be in.

He said, quietly, *The military is full of tricks.*

He began to see another side of the Military.

Having that being said, on Friday of the first week that he attended that school, he went to see his captain.

"Captain, I had spoken to my sergeant this past Monday. I told him that I didn't sign up for the Correctional Specialist School and that I wanted to be released from it. He told me to wait until today to come and tell you," John said.

"Soldier, I'm sorry to hear that you want to be released from the school. Unfortunately, it's a little bit too late. You should have come to me on the first day," he said.

John shook his head in disbelief. He had gotten a taste of *the military system of things.* He then realized that he had to adapt and learn a new game. He decided to make the best of it.

John completed that course, and he was given his new military orders. The military had ordered him to attend a Military Police Intelligence School. He was able to get out of that one.

However, after doing so, and as time passed, he began to think whether or not he had made a mistake by not going to that school. He believed the military had plans for him.

He also believed in the possibility that it may not have been what the Lord had in mind for him to do. If so, he probably wouldn't have been able to get out of going to that school either.

John was ordered to report to Fort Campbell, and upon his arrival, a sergeant approached him and the others that had come.

"My name is Sergeant Lewis. I want to welcome you all here. You will be assigned to work in the stockade," the sergeant said.

"I didn't join the Army to work in a stockade," John said out loud so that the sergeant could hear him.

The sergeant stared at John and then very sincerely said, "Private, all you have to do is to stick it out for one week, and if you don't like it after that, you can go to the captain. The captain will take care of it for you."

"Sergeant, I have heard that one before," John said boldly and out loud.

That remark really made the sergeant mad. John could tell by the expression on his face. John didn't waste his time by going to his captain.

Having that being said, and as fate would have it, as time passed, John believed he had become a marked man.

Everyone that had come with him when he had first arrived was being promoted. He wasn't promoted. He still had his mosquito wings, which meant he was still a private.

John hadn't done anything wrong. He deserved to have been promoted too. He took that as a sign that he wasn't going to be treated fairly, and he knew he had a long way to go to fulfill his enlistment contract.

Having that being said and as time passed, John thought about a bunion that had developed on both of his feet that became agitated and would hurt when he wore his army boots and shoes for a long period of time. His ego had prevented him from complaining about it before. He toughed it out.

Having that being said, John decided to complain about it. He made an appointment to go and see a doctor.

"Doctor, I have a problem with my feet. I noticed that my feet would hurt when I wore my boots and shoes for a long period of time," John complained.

The doctor had two braces made for John to put in his boots and shoes. The braces were made to ease the pain.

"Soldier, put these braces in your boots and in your shoes, and report back to me in two weeks for further evaluation," the doctor said.

Having that being said, the two weeks went by pretty fast. John returned back to the doctor's office and said, "Doctor, the braces didn't work. My feet still hurt."

"I'm sorry to hear that," the doctor said. "I'm going to issue you a medical profile stating that you can't wear hard sole shoes for no longer than two to three hours a day," he said.

It was just what he wanted to hear. There was a big smile on his face.

John went and bought himself a brand-new white pair of Converse tennis shoes. He wore them while he was in uniform.

"They want to play games. Well, the game is on," he said with a smile on his face.

John remembered going to the mess hall. He went to the chow line to get his food. He noticed while he was walking toward a table, there were several soldiers looking at his tennis shoes.

Having that being said, a sergeant trying to impress his superiors approached John and said, "Soldier, why are you out of uniform?"

John acted as if he didn't hear him.

"Soldier, why are you out of uniform?" he said again very loudly as to get the attention of his superiors and others.

John still didn't say anything. He just smiled as he reached into his shirt pocket. He showed the sergeant his medical profile.

The sergeant became motionless while reading John's medical profile. He couldn't do anything but to leave John alone. The sergeant was upset and embarrassed. The sergeant walked away from John.

After John had finished eating, he reported to work as if nothing was wrong and/or had happened.

Then all of a sudden, Sergeant Lewis approached him. John could tell that he was mad. He must have been told what had taken place in the mess hall.

"Soldier, you are out of uniform," he said loudly.

John didn't waste any time with him. He reached into his pocket to retrieve his medical profile, and he showed it to him.

The sergeant held it in his hand and was shaking his head as he stared at it without saying a word. He appeared to be mumbling to himself.

He finally said, "We can't have you walking around in uniform like this. I want you to report to the barrack and wait for further instructions."

"Yes, sir, Sergeant," John said with a smile on his face as he headed toward the barrack.

John couldn't wait to get back to the barrack. He sat down on his bunk, and then he laid down on his bunk, which just so happen to be the top bunk. He smiled as he looked at his brand-new tennis shoes. He was anticipating and wondering what was going to happen next.

It didn't take long before Sergeant Lewis arrived. He approached John. John rose from his bed. He didn't respect his sergeant enough to have gone through the trouble of getting out of the bed.

"Soldier, until further notice, you will be assigned to the barrack as a barracks orderly," he said in a demanding tone of voice. "Sergeant Nightwind will be your immediate supervisor."

Having that being said, John was upset at first, and as time passed, he began to like his new assignment. It turned out to be great. He was off on the weekends and holidays, and the job wasn't that hard. The only two problems he had was the fact that he still hadn't been promoted, and he didn't join the Army to be a barracks orderly.

In the meantime, John decided to file a grievance. He went to see a JAG officer. The JAG officer was a lawyer for the army's legal department.

"I didn't join the Army to become a barracks orderly, and I hadn't done anything wrong for me not to have been promoted. It wasn't my fault that I have a medical profile," John said as he complained to the JAG officer.

"By looking at your record and your history, I find no reason why you shouldn't have been promoted and why you were assigned as a barracks orderly. I will notify your company commanding officer. I will order your captain to report back to me. Come back to see me in two weeks," the JAG officer said.

"Yes, sir," John responded with a smile on his face.

He couldn't wait for the two weeks to pass.

Having that being said, two weeks later, John reported back to the JAG officer.

The JAG officer said, "Private Robinson, your commanding officer had failed to get back with me. I will file an order for him to reply, and I'll notify you of a hearing date."

Having that being said, and being that John wasn't performing his duties according to the agreement the recruiter and he had originally agreed too, he decided to let his hair grow out. His hair was long enough to be braided. John made plans to get his hair braided.

He hadn't seen a soldier with his hair braided before, specifically while in uniform. He knew there weren't a policy and/or a military order that said that he couldn't have his hair braided while in uniform.

It just so happened John had gone home on a particular weekend, he had his sister-in-law to braid his hair, and he returned back to his barrack on a Sunday night.

On the following Monday, a Black sergeant approached John and said, "Soldier, what's wrong with your hair?"

John responded by saying, "There is nothing wrong with my hair."

The sergeant then ordered John to report to their commanding officer.

"Sir, this soldier is violating the Military Dress Code," the sergeant said to their captain.

The captain was sitting at his desk at the time. He stood up and approached John. He looked at John's hair and said, "You are violating the Military Dress Code."

"No, sir. I am not violating the dress code," John said very calmly.

The captain went and got the military order that pertained to haircuts. He looked at several pictures of Black soldiers.

"Captain, there isn't anything said about braids. Therefore, it can't be proven and/or said that I was violating the Military Dress Code. However, to keep confusion down, I will take down my braids, sir," John said in attempt to show his willingness to be a team player.

As time passed, John had discovered that the military orders pertaining to haircuts had been changed to reflect that a male soldier couldn't have his hair braided while in uniform.

In the meantime, he was advised to report to the JAG Office. He wore a fresh starched uniform, and he wore his tennis shoes. He was still playing the game.

Upon his arrival, he noticed that there were quite a few high-ranking officers in a hearing room. He was told to wait until he was called.

He was finally called. He looked at all of them before he said anything. He knew his future was on the line. His heart seemed to be beating fast.

Then he said, "It is with regret that I am forced to be here today. It was never my intention. I joined the Army to serve my country as a military policeman, and they assigned me to work in a stockade against my wishes. They wouldn't promote me. I haven't done anything wrong, and they made me a barracks orderly."

"Why can't we just assign him to work in a recreational unit?" one officer said.

"He has to be an E-4 and/or a sergeant in order for us to do that. He is just an E-1," another officer said.

"Well, Private Robinson, what is it that you want us to do?" the highest-ranking officer said.

That was John's clue. It was what he had hoped someone would have asked him.

John said, in a very emotional tone of voice, "As I had mentioned to you before, I regret having been placed in this predicament. I had joined to serve my country, and now with your permission, I would like to be released from that obligation, sir."

"We will take that under consideration. You will be notified in the next few days of our decision," the highest-ranking officer said.

A week later, John received his new military orders. He hesitated for a few minutes before he read the military order. He remembered saying, "This is it! It's what I have been waiting on."

It said, "Private Robinson, your request to be discharged from the United States Army is granted. You will be honorably discharged within three days from the date of this letter, and all benefits will be afforded to you."

After reading the military order, John wasn't as happy as he thought he would have been. He was actually sad. He didn't have an exit game plan. He really didn't want to get out of the Army. He actually had another year to go on his contract. He then began to think about what he was going to do next.

Having that being said, in John's vision, he remembered saying to himself, *All I wanted was to be treated fair and to have been told the truth.*

Book Five

TSU

John was only twenty years old when he was honorably discharged from the Army. He had married his girlfriend, and they had a son. John named him John Jr.

John wasn't old enough to become a state trooper. As a result, he decided to go to college instead. He was accepted at TSU, which was considered to be a historical Black college.

Having that being said, Black history wasn't taught that much to John when he attended military schools as a child. In fact, it wasn't taught that much to him when he attended civilian schools.

His major was in criminal justice. Psychology and sociology were his minors.

As fate would have it, and as time passed, John had learned more about the history and struggles of the Black man than he ever had before.

It turned out that history had become one of John's favorite subjects, and the events that had taken place during the civil rights movement had gotten his attention. It must have touched a nerve of his.

As fate would have it, several of John's professors had taken an interest in him.

Dr. Wheaton said, "John, I want you to do your research paper on Rev. Martin Luther King Jr. and Malcolm X. I want you to compare the two."

John didn't know that much about them until he had finished his research paper. He felt he had something in common with both of them. He understood them both. He respected them, and he was glad to have been given that assignment.

He believed he had the heart of Rev. Martin Luther King Jr. and the mind of Malcolm X.

Having that being said, he believed it was the Lord's will for him to know more about the historical background and the struggles of the Black race as well as other minorities, specifically in America.

The more John learned about the historical background and the struggle of the Black man, the more he realized what he hadn't been taught.

For some reason, John had a different perspective from what he believed he was expected to believe and understand by the mere reading of the words written in the books he had read.

He believed the Lord wanted him to look beyond the words and to see and understand the contents spiritually.

Having that being said, John believed the Founding Fathers, who were involved in the drafting of the United States Constitution, the Bill of Rights, and the laws of the land in their time, weren't written originally for the benefit of the Black man at all. He believed their intentions and purpose for the Black man was to be a slave and nothing more.

Having that being said, other than the Lord's will, John believed if it weren't for the civil rights movement, the Founding Father's ideas, attitude, and behavior wouldn't have changed, specifically toward the Black man.

John believed in the course of time, the civil rights movement had forced society and the government to accept the fact that the same benefits should be afforded to the Black man as well.

John truly believed the concept and the idea of calling a Black man an African American had a hidden agenda, and it served a deeper sinister purpose.

He believed calling a Black man an African American had racial overtones and nothing to do with respect for the Black race and/

or its heritage. He believed it was a way for the racist individuals in America, with a smile on their face, to slander the Black man.

He believed if it hadn't been for the racial discrimination lawsuits that had been filed and won in the court of law, referring to a Black man as the N-word would still be acceptable and said in public as well as it still being continually said behind closed doors.

So therefore, he believed and had come to the conclusion that it would be easier for the racist individuals in America's society to get away with calling a Black man an African than it would have been to call a Black man the N-word.

He based his analogy upon remembering and hearing with his own ears some of them say to the Black man, "Why don't you go back to Africa where you belong?"

That alone in John's opinion should have raised the awareness and the actual intent and reason behind referring to a Black man as an African American.

He also believed, as a result of the civil rights movement, certain political positions within the city, state, and federal government as well as within the civilian society had been strategically made available to certain civil rights leaders.

As a result, John believed once the majority of them had obtained certain positions within the general public and the government, and having been exposed to the life style of those positions of power, and status, the majority of them had become more concerned with their title and position.

Having that being said, John believed they had forgotten where they came from. In other words, he believed the majority of them had sold their souls to the system, and as a result, they had accepted the title and concept of being called the new N-word, "African American."

John refused to consider himself as being and/or referred to as being an African American. He wasn't born in Africa. He was born in America.

As fate would have it, another professor had taken an interest in John and said, "John, I want you to do your research paper on ancient law."

John really didn't know where to begin. He remembered starting out by reading the King James Version of the Bible, Greek mythology, and several of his criminal justice books.

As a result thereof, he had learned a great deal about the origin of law and how it began and the effects of it. He felt there must have been a reason why he was chosen to do those research papers. He believed the Lord had something to do with it.

Having that being said, as time passed, John turned twenty-one years old. He had to quit going to school. He needed a job to help support his family.

He remembered submitting an application to the Metropolitan Police Department. He knew politics was involved in the hiring process as well as the color of his skin. He wasn't hired.

He then submitted an application to the Department of Corrections. He knew he really didn't want to work in a prison. However, he needed a job.

As fate would have it, John was notified to appear at the main prison to be interviewed.

He remembered sitting in the lobby. He said quietly, *Do I really want to work with those prisoners? Do I really want to be behind those prison walls all day with them?*

John's name was called.

"Mr. Robinson," the interviewer said.

John stood up and said, "I'm Mr. Robinson. I also want you to know that I really appreciate the opportunity that you have given me to be interviewed. I have thought about it. I have decided not to go forward with this interview. Thank you very much."

John then walked out of the lobby.

As fate would have it, a week later, he received a letter from the Department of Corrections.

"Mr. Robinson, we want to thank you for your honesty. We would like for you to consider working with our youth within our juvenile institutions," the letter said.

Hmm! They may have a point, John remembered saying to himself. He believed the Lord had a hand in that.

As fate would have it, he was hired and assigned to Spencer Youth Center. SYC was a juvenile correctional institution located in Nashville.

Book Six

Spencer Youth Center

John remembered the very first day he arrived to work at SYC. He was assigned to work the 4:00 p.m. to 12:00 p.m. shift. He was assigned to be a relief dormitory supervisor, which meant when a dormitory supervisor needed to take a break, he would have to supervise their dormitory during their break.

A dormitory supervisor's responsibility was to supervise the students within their dormitory. The dormitory supervisor was responsible for the well-being of their students.

The juveniles were called students, and the institution was referred to as being a campus.

Being a relief dormitory supervisor, in John's opinion, was very stressful and nonproductive. The students knew he was new, and he wasn't their main dormitory supervisor.

"Hey, guys! We got ourselves a rookie. Let's give him a hard time," John heard a student say.

Several students asked him to do things for them that they knew he weren't supposed to do, and they gave him a hard time by not immediately following his instructions.

It seemed like to John that he had been prepared in advance. He was already exposed to such tactics, and the more he remembered and thought about that in his vision, the more he believed the Lord had him just where he wanted him to be.

John's Military Police and Correctional Specialist Training, and the fact that he had worked in a stockade, had also come in handy. He did the unexpected. He wrote them up for trying to manipulate staff and for not following his instructions.

A write-up consisted of a dormitory supervisor's written notes pertaining to negative and inappropriate behavior. A student would have to appear before a due process hearing as a result of a write-up. The student could lose a certain amount of points as a result of a write-up.

A student had to earn a certain amount of point's to be released from the institution. A student had to earn those points per week, and if that student didn't earn enough points per week, that student would not have earned a week's stay at the institution. It would have been like the student wasn't there. In other words, the student would have wasted one week of time.

John had noticed a veteran dormitory supervisor, who, for some reason, had to relieve another dormitory supervisor, wouldn't go to the extreme of writing up a student.

He became the exception, and he wasn't considered being a veteran dormitory supervisor. That caught the other dormitory supervisors and their students by surprise.

"Man! He wrote me up! He wrote me up too," John heard a student tell another student.

The word had gotten out that John wasn't cool, and he would write them up for nothing.

John knew how the game was played. His plan of action was to establish a reputation of being hard to manipulate as well the fact that he would write them up. His plan was put to the test on his very first night.

As time passed, several weeks had gone by. John remembered hearing a rumor that he was going to be assigned to York Dormitory.

York Dormitory was considered the hardest dormitory for a supervisor to work in. He heard that the dormitory supervisors that were assigned to that dormitory really didn't care about their students, and the dormitory manager was gay. John was hoping that he wouldn't be assigned to that dormitory.

Having that being said, it seemed like more students were sent to the Control Unit from York Dormitory than any other dormitory on campus.

It just so happened he had been assigned to work in the Control Unit. That was one way how he knew what dormitory the students had come from.

The Control Unit was isolated away from the other dormitories on purpose. It was like a jail. It had about eight individual small rooms made of concrete and iron bars. The Control Unit was also called The Cells.

It was where students were sent to as a result of their negative behavior and/or punishment as a result of a due process hearing.

There were also more students housed in York Dormitory than any other dormitory, and it was connected to a dormitory called Prerelease.

The students that were assigned to the Prerelease Dormitory were the ones who had earned enough points in their regular dormitory to be sent to the Prerelease Dormitory.

Being sent to the Prerelease Dormitory was the last stage a student had to go through prior to being released from the institution. Those students had special privileges and were the only students on campus that were able to be unsupervised when they were outside their dormitory and while out on the campus grounds.

On many occasions, the dormitory supervisor of York Dormitory would have to supervise the Prerelease Dormitory as well, and at times, there would be ten to twenty students assigned to that dormitory.

As fate would have it, in less than two months, John was assigned to York Dormitory. In a way, he knew he was going to be.

He replaced Jack. Jack was assigned to work on the security detail. He was an army veteran and was the leader of the social click that was there. He had a lot of followers, including supervisors that were over him and John.

Mr. Garner was the dormitory manager. He introduced John to the students.

There were about twenty-three students in the dormitory at that time. It was more than the allotted number of students to be in one dormitory according to state regulations.

John remembered standing before them. He actually felt sorry for them. They looked like they had gone through hell. One could hear a pin drop. They were waiting on John to say something. They had already heard about his reputation. John was counting on that.

"My name is John D. Robinson. I want you all to know that the rumor you may have heard that I would write you up is true. Having that being said, as time pass, you will find out that I will become your best friend once you get to know me. All that I expect you to do is to follow my instructions. You follow my instructions, and everything will be okay. You will see," John said in a fatherly tone of voice.

John noticed that the dormitory supervisor's desk was in front of the dormitory facing the students and the back door. The television was on the wall over and behind the desk.

He didn't like that arrangement. He decided to reorganize the seating arrangements and a few other things to benefit him. He placed the desk just behind the back of the students. That way, the students couldn't see what he would be doing.

Having that being said, he could see what they were doing, which, in his opinion, would keep them wondering what he was doing.

He instructed them to raise their hand if they wanted permission to do something.

John figured if they didn't raise their hand and would turn around to look to see what he was doing, it would be an indication that they might be up to something.

He assigned students who he felt he could somewhat trust to be closer to his desk.

In the meantime, Jack had been telling his followers that John wasn't going to last three months. They all had laughed about it. It was apparent that John wasn't one of Jack's followers, and Jack didn't like that.

As time passed, specifically after the three-month deadline that Jack had given John, John had become very popular and respected among his students as well as many of the other students on campus. He became York's main dormitory supervisor.

That didn't set to, well, among several of John's peers, and the majority of them were surprised.

The majority of the other dormitory supervisors as well as their supervisors became envious of John, especially when some of their own student's would say to them, "How come you can't be like Mr. Robinson?"

John heard them say that on several occasions when his students and their students crossed paths.

John's students as well as some of the other students on campus would use his name as a way of having fun and to make other students and supervisors mad.

As time passed, John began writing up a lot of students that weren't in his dormitory. He did that for several reasons. He wanted the other students on campus to know that it didn't make any difference where they were and whether or not they were with their own supervisors. He would write them up if they acted inappropriately when his students and he were present.

He did that in attempt to prevent students from other dormitories from getting his students involved in inappropriate behavior. The slang term was called gassing up.

He became known as the Time Taker, and as a result, his students and he became somewhat popular throughout the campus.

Having that being said, students throughout the campus began to come to him as a result of them being written up by their supervisors. John had become their advocate of choice.

John really didn't mind representing them during their disciplinary hearings. He would usually capitalize on the mistakes that their supervisors would make in their write-ups. It was John's way of getting back at those supervisors who had been trying to give him a hard time.

As years passed, John had discovered that there were students who wanted to be assigned to his dormitory. The students that were already in his dormitory were proud to be in York Dormitory. They would often brag about it.

For some reason, John believed the administration was trying to put a lot of pressure on him. He began to notice that students who had displayed constant inappropriate behavior in the other dormitories were being transferred to his dormitory.

He remembered there were four eighteen-year-old students from another institution that were accused of starting a riot. SYC didn't house eighteen-year-olds.

Their institution's administrators needed to get them away from their institution. The administrators needed time to get things back in order and in control. The rumor was that those students were going to be temporarily transferred to SYC.

Having that being said, every one of the dormitory supervisors and managers at SYC were wondering who were going to get them. They didn't want those students in their dormitory and neither did John.

Those students were the ones who were too old to be at a juvenile institution like SYC, and the majority of them were waiting to be sent to an adult correctional institution. John knew he was going to get at least one of them.

As fate would have it, not one but all four of them were placed in his dormitory. Their size, attitude, and demeanor intimidated John's students as well as the other dormitory supervisors and managers.

John *imagined* them all saying among themselves, *I am glad that Robinson got them instead of us. He is going to have problems with them. He won't be able to handle them.*

Having that being said, John believed they were hoping something bad would happen so that they could have something to talk about.

He suspected that those four students thought he also was going to be intimidated. They had let him know from the very beginning that they were upset because they had been sent to SYC. They looked at SYC as being a place for kids. They did have a point. They were correct.

Needless to say, John was upset too. He wasn't upset at them. He was upset because of the fact that the administration purposely had singled him out as the one to get all of them.

John took note and advantage of what those four students didn't like.

He instructed them to sit down in front of his desk. John's students were quiet and were waiting on him to do and/or to say something to them. One could hear a pin drop.

John remembered looking at the four of them. He looked straight into their eyes and said in a stern tone of voice, "My name is John D. Robinson. I know you would prefer not to be here. You have already made that clear. But, yet, you are here!

"You were sent here as a result of being accused of starting a riot at the institution where you had come from. I want you to know that I understand how you must feel, and I know you can't wait to get back there.

"However, in the meantime, you are here now. You are older guys. I expect you to be more mature than my students. I expect you to follow my instructions. If you do that, you will find your stay here tolerable.

"On the other hand, if you don't follow my instructions, you will find that I will become your worst nightmare.

"There is a reason why all of you were placed in my dormitory. Think about that! I will write you up, and I will do everything within my power to keep you here. You will find yourself stuck here until you had satisfied the punishment that your inappropriate behavior might cause if you chose to go that route.

"It's all up to you. I will respect you, and I will treat you fair. All you have to do is to follow my instructions."

As fate would have it, those students were transferred back to their institution four days later. John never did have a problem with them.

John could only *imagine* how his peers felt after discovering that he didn't have any problems with them. He knew they wouldn't have admitted that he was a better supervisor than they were.

As time passed, John no longer worked the 4:00 p.m. to 12:00 p.m. shift on Saturday and Sunday. He worked 8:00 a.m. to 4:00 p.m.

As fate would have it, John had been noticing that quite a few of his peers had been receiving letters stating how good of a job they have been doing, and a few of them were promoted.

He also noticed that those letters were given to the individuals that were within the social click instead of the individuals who weren't and whom he thought really deserved them.

In spite of all the hard work he had been doing and what the administration had been putting him through during his past five years of employment, he hadn't received a letter stating what a good job he had been doing.

John knew what was going on. Those demons of the system were trying to make him mad. They successfully succeeded. He was mad and upset about it. He wrote a letter to an administrator expressing his concern. His name was Randall.

John said, "Mr. Randall, I am writing you this letter to say that I feel like I am being looked over and not being given a fair evaluation as for the good work that I have contributed to this institution. I admit I had received a favorable evaluation from my dormitory manager but not from the administration.

"I have noticed that you had given quite a few of your friends complementary letters, and some of them had been promoted. I just wanted to let you know that it was unfair."

As fate would have it, the following day, John was given a letter stating what a good job he had been doing.

He had to admit, Mr. Randall did try to make him feel better. However, the letter wasn't good enough for John. In his opinion, that letter was too late in coming. He believed it was only given to him because of his complaint.

John had that letter with him when he went to talk to Mr. Randall. It was perfect timing. A few good old boys were in his office when he walked in. Jack was one of them.

John didn't say a word to them. He balled up the letter in front of them and threw it in the trash can as he walked out of the office.

John knew there would be a possibility of them retaliating against him. But it didn't matter to him.

Having that being said, and as time passed, the administration started using his dormitory as a training dormitory for the new dormitory supervisors. They were only being trained while on his shift and when he was working.

John didn't like the fact that he was being used and the fact that he wasn't being paid for training them.

Having that being said, John had a lot going on in his personal life as well. He had another son. His name was Antonio. He named him after his younger brother who, at the time, didn't have any kids. John had also gone back to college.

John began to think more about his education. He felt having a degree would enhance his chances of getting promoted and/or to get a better-paying job. In other words, he was looking for a way out.

He felt himself getting burned out. The demons were constantly putting pressure on him.

He *imagined* them saying, behind closed doors, *I believe we got him now. He won't last much longer. He'll break down soon.*

Needless to say, they were just about right. He was at the point of giving up.

John remembered thinking about his life again and tears formed in his eyes.

He prayed and said, "Lord, why is it that I always catch hell? I caught hell in the Military, and I am catching hell here. Why won't I just bow down to them and do what they do? Who am I?"

As fate would have it, for some reason, he had an urge to get his King James Version of the Bible.

He got his Bible, and then he laid down in his bed. He held his Bible within the palms of his hands. The Bible was closed. The pages were facing his face.

He closed his eyes, and he said, "Lord, if you are trying to tell me something, let it be."

He then relaxed his hands so that the Bible would open up freely. The Bible had opened up to the very first page of Ecclesiastes.

Having that being said, he thought about the odds of that happening. He knew the Lord had to have had something to do with that.

For some reason, he had an urge to read out loud. Normally, he would have read silently.

As John began to read the book of Ecclesiastes, it seemed like to him that the tone of his voice was changing. It sounded deeper than he had ever heard before. He liked the way he was sounding. He continued reading out loud.

It seemed like to John that someone else was reading the book of Ecclesiastes to him. He believed it was the Lord's voice that he was hearing. He believed the Lord had used his voice as his. He believed the Lord was answering him as he read the book of Ecclesiastes.

He believed that was how he had come up with the saying "I don't believe in coincidences. I believe there is a reason for everything and nothing happens by chance."

John believed after reading the book of Ecclesiastes, he might have been chosen to be one of the Lord's messengers. He believed everything that he had gone through up to that point in his vision was to make him stronger mentally and spiritually.

Having that being said, the following night, a strange thing had happened to him. He had always had a phobia about sleeping on his back. It reminded him of a person being in a coffin, and every time he would find himself in that position, he would turn over and sleep on his side and/or his stomach.

For some reason, that night he didn't care. He drifted off to sleep or so he thought.

As he slept, he realized that he could see his eyelash. He then wondered, and he thought, *If I can see my eyelashes, my eyes must have been opened. I must not have been asleep.*

When he came to that conclusion, he realized that something had to have happened to him. He woke up, and he felt great. He couldn't explain it. He tried to figure it out. He believed he had a phenomenal experience.

John wondered if he could experience that same feeling again. He couldn't wait for the next night to come.

As fate would have it, that night had come. John was excited, and he laid down on his back again. He drifted off to sleep.

He remembered, as he slept, he heard a sound in both of his eardrums that sounded like an airplane engine revving up in preparation to take off. The sound had gotten louder, louder, and louder. It had reached the point where an airplane would have normally taken off and it didn't. The sound kept on getting louder and louder.

He thought his head was going to burst wide open. He panicked. He knew something was wrong, and he thought that he was going to die in his sleep.

He tried to speak to his wife. He wanted to tell her what was going on with him, and when he couldn't speak to her, he tried to scream. He couldn't do that either.

Lord! Help me! Help me! Whatever I am going through, please help me come out of it, he said frantically.

John immediately came out of the state of mind that he found himself in. He was sweating and breathing faster. He then realized and thought that he was playing a dangerous game. He believed he had tapped into the spiritual realm.

As time passed, John thought about those two experiences. He realized that his first experience was by accident or so he thought. He enjoyed it. His second experience was intentional, and it liked to have scared him to death.

As a result, he became curious. He went to a local library to check out a few books about ESP (extrasensory perception).

He never did read the books in depth. He just glanced through the pages.

John remembered, as time passed, he noticed that students started to come to him from all over the campus. They wanted to talk to him. They began to tell him things that they wouldn't tell their own dormitory supervisors and/or their dormitory managers. They said they didn't even tell the preachers that would come to their dormitories on Sunday mornings.

Having that being said, and speaking of preachers, he felt he needed to be saved. He didn't want to take any chances as a result of his past spiritual experiences. He asked the preacher that came to his dormitory to meet with him at the back door of the dormitory one Sunday morning.

"Preacher, I want to be saved," John said.

"Do you accept Jesus Christ as your Savior?" the preacher asked.

"Yes, I do," John replied.

For some reason, he was expecting to feel different. He didn't remember feeling any differently than he did prior to being saved. But he was glad that he went through the process anyway.

As fate would have it, John became concerned about some of the things the students had told him. As far as he knew, they didn't hold back anything. They told him about some problems they had experienced within their families and friends.

They talked about their drug and alcohol use when they had committed offenses and crimes, which, in his opinion, was the ultimate determining factor that led them to being incarcerated.

It just so happened a local television station had been reporting about crimes being committed by juveniles, and some officials of the Department of Youth Development had been asked questions that pertained to that problem.

As fate would have it, John was instructed by his professor in one of his criminal justice classes to do a research paper. He didn't know what he was going to do it on.

Having that being said, that night, John was thinking about what he was going to do his research paper on as he drifted off to sleep.

In his vision, he saw himself having a vision, and in his vision, he saw children dying as a result of drugs and alcohol abuse. And somehow, it felt like to him that those children were actually his. He felt the pain of a grieved parent.

In his mind and in his heart, those children had actually taken the place of his natural children. He loved them in spite of being the authoritative figure over them. He loved them as a father, as a brother, as a friend, and in some cases like a mother.

He saw himself crying out to the Lord, and he said, "Lord, what is it that I can do to help save the children?"

As he thought about it, he believed that question was what the Lord was waiting on him to ask.

John *imagined* hearing an Angel of the Lord saying to him, *The Lord wants you to conduct a research paper pertaining to drugs and alcohol abuse among those children at SYC.*

John then *imagined* hearing another voice saying to him, *I must show you the one who is responsible for the destruction of my father's children.*

John suddenly visualized seeing himself in a dark room. It was so dark that he couldn't see his own hand in front of him. He was afraid, and he was trembling. He didn't move.

Then all of a sudden, he saw a light a short distant away from where he was. That light was very dim. He could barely see it. It was similar to a light that would be seen on a lit candle.

He saw himself walking very slowly and nervously toward that light, and as he got closer to the light, the light appeared to take on an image of a man with his back turned toward him. The man was wearing what it appeared to him to be a robe.

He saw himself grabbing hold to the robe. He suddenly felt safe. It was as if he was in the presence of the Lord. He believed it was the Lord.

He *imagined* seeing the Lord walking forward. He noticed that he could only see what was in front of the Lord.

John was curious. He thought he had seen a glimpse of an image that was hiding in the dark. He peeked out from behind the Lord's back so that he could get a better look.

He stepped out from behind the light, and he believed he was spotted by that image. The image that he had seen had frightened him.

He hid back behind the Lord, hoping that he wasn't seen by that image but yet thinking that he must have been seen. He believed the imaged that he had seen was Satan himself.

Suddenly, a thought came to his mind. He remembered saying to himself, *so that's it! It's Satan. What better way for the Great Deceiver of the world to destroy the world than to destroy the children? A world without children cannot survive.* The thought made a lot of sense to him.

John remembered saying, "Lord, how in the world am I going to be able to get away with doing that research paper? You know someone from the administration comes through my dormitory all the time. You know they have been trying to find a way to fire me."

John was expecting a response from the Lord. He didn't receive one, at least to his knowledge.

"Okay then! If it is your *will*, let it be done," John said.

John set out to prove that drug and alcohol abuse caused criminal behavior, and as a result of that behavior, a child would be addicted, suicidal, incarcerated, and/or killed.

He asked his students if they wanted to participate in his research project, and every one of them volunteered. They felt that it was an honor to be involved.

As fate would have it, John noticed during the first month when he decided to work on his research paper, no one from the administration would come in his dormitory. He knew then that the Lord wasn't going to let anyone interfere with his project.

It took several months for him to finally finish his research paper, and as soon as he had put the last period on the last word of the sentence, someone from the administration came in his dormitory.

John saw himself smiling, and he said, "Man, I had gotten away with it."

Having that being said, John really didn't realize what he had actually done and/or had started. He thought he was killing two birds with one stone, meaning he was doing what the Lord wanted him to do, and he was getting a grade for it at the same time.

After he had thought about it, he had come to the conclusion that his research paper was deeper than what he had originally thought and expected. He believed he had opened Pandora's box.

As a result of his research paper, he discovered that the majority of his students had committed a criminal offense while under the influence of drugs and/or alcohol. He also discovered that a lot of them had obtained drugs and/or alcohol while they were incarcerated.

John thought he had discovered a problem that the commissioner of Department of Corrections as well as the commissioner of the Department of Youth Development would have been appreciative of.

He gave the director of SYC a copy of his research paper. He thought that the director was going to be appreciative. He was wrong. The director didn't respond.

He then sent the commissioner of the Department of Youth Development a copy of his research paper. The commissioner didn't respond either.

John came to the conclusion that the majority of the government officials within the Department of Corrections and the Department of Youth Development, who had said they were concerned about the drug and alcohol problem among juveniles, really didn't care about the problem at all. They, in his opinion, had misled the media and public into thinking they were really concerned about the problem.

He believed they were more concerned with detention than prevention as detention brought more funds into the system and under the table, and prevention would have slowed down that flow of funds.

He then sent Governor Alexander a copy of his research paper and a proposal to allow him to conduct a similar research paper within the other juvenile and adult correctional institutions.

As fate would have it, the governor responded within two weeks and said, "Mr. Robinson, I found your research paper very interesting. I appreciate an employee such as you taking the time to conduct a research paper pertaining to the problem of drug and alcohol abuse among our juveniles. I am going to send your study and request to the commissioner for him to assist you in your project."

John was glad to have received the governor's letter. He knew then that Commissioner Long wasn't going to be happy. He knew the commissioner was going to respond after that.

Sure enough, he immediately received a letter from the commissioner saying, "Dear Mr. Robinson, I had received a copy of your research paper and proposal from the governor. I have found some of the things you said to be very helpful. However, in the near future, don't do anything like this again without getting my permission first. As for assisting you in your project, I'll allow you to take a one-year leave of absence without pay."

John couldn't afford to take a leave of absence without pay. He felt like the commissioner had threatened him indirectly. John knew then that the target on his back had gotten bigger.

As time passed, he heard that the Department of Corrections and the Department of Youth Development had suddenly started conducting random searches for contraband throughout all of its institutions except for SYC.

He believed they didn't want him to know he had touched a nerve of theirs.

John also noticed that the Department of Corrections as well as several other state departments had revised some of their programs and procedures that dealt with probation, youth services, and their Drug and Alcohol Programs.

Their new programs seemed to have had similar characteristic as to what John had proposed. It just didn't have his name on it as the author.

As time passed, John could tell that he was being watched. He believed every move that he had made was being scrutinized as if someone was waiting on him to make a mistake.

He thought about sending the letter that he had received from the commissioner to the governor.

However, he decided that it wouldn't be to his best interest. He was afraid of the consequences, and as a result, that didn't set well with him knowing that he was afraid.

Having that being said, that was one of the reasons why he decided to take martial arts. He believed in the philosophy of Bruce Lee. Bruce Lee was a well-known martial artist. The sport focused on being able to utilize one's ability to concentrate as well as other things.

John had planned on perfecting his ability to concentrate. He wanted to be able to conquer fear by using his mind.

He brought a picture of a black panther. The panther looked as if it was about to attack someone or something.

John thought the black panther was the most feared animal in the jungle. He thought if he could concentrate enough to be able to kill the panther with his bare hands mentally, he wouldn't be afraid of anything.

As time passed, he decided to test his theory. His wife and kids were asleep. He went to his spare room, which he referred to as being his Room of Solitude. The picture of the panther was placed on the door on the inside of the room.

He sat quietly on the floor with his legs crossed together. His plan was not to close his eyes while staring into the eyes of the panther.

Having that being said, it seemed like it only took a few minutes. In John's mind, it seemed like the panther was beginning to move toward him.

He imagined hearing every step that it made. It sounded like something was walking on a wooded floor that squeaked.

John jumped up and screamed. He thought the panther was about to attack him. His ability to conquer fear mentally didn't work.

As fate would have it, a familiar sensation came upon him. He *imagined* hearing a voice say to him very sternly, *John, if you were without fear, then you wouldn't fear me.* John understood.

He then realized that he had the ability to tap into the spiritual realm.

Having that being said, as time passed, John hadn't learned his lesson. He had a notion to use his newly acquired ability to see if he could see God spiritually.

He remembered the night he decided to see if he could tap into the spiritual realm in order to see if he could see God.

He was lying down in his bed. He was facing the ceiling fan as he drifted off to sleep. As he slept he had a vision and in his vision he saw himself looking at his own body as it lay on the bed.

As he looked at his body he believed he saw a spirit which looked like the shape of a human body. The spirit was rising out of his body.

It seemed like to him that there were two entities. One was himself, which somehow enabled him to see the spirit, and the other was the spirit itself.

Having that being said, John referred to himself as being him in the physical sense.

John noticed the spirit that he was looking at began to travel upward, and somehow he was able to follow it. The spirit went through what appeared to be a tunnel, and as the spirit traveled upward in the tunnel it appeared to get darker and darker inside the tunnel. It had gotten to the point where he was only able to see the darkness and nothing else. He didn't see that spirit anymore.

Having that being said, John noticed that he was still traveling upward in the tunnel. He then noticed that it started to get lighter and lighter, and then brighter and brighter.

Then all of sudden, it was as if he had crashed into something, which caused him to come to an abrupt halt.

It seemed like to him that he had crashed into a bright light. It was as if the light of a camera's flash bulb had flashed in front of his eyes. It blinded him. He couldn't see anything.

Then all of a sudden, he noticed that he was falling backward toward his body at a very high rate of speed.

Somehow, he knew he had entered into his body. Somehow, he felt that something was about to go wrong. He knew he needed to come back to reality and it had to happen quickly.

Having that being said, while inside of his body John was able to hear his vital organs functioning. He could hear the fluids flowing within his body. He could hear his own heart beating.

Then all of a sudden, while still being inside of his own body he realized that his human sense, meaning his mind, was trying to figure out what was going on. Somehow John knew that he couldn't let his mind focus to the point of figuring out what was happening. He felt if his mind had solved the mystery of what was going on while he was still inside of his own body, somehow it would have caused him to be in a coma, and he would have been trapped.

Having that being said, John knew then that he had gone too far into the spiritual realm for his own good, and that was when he said, "Lord, whatever is going on, please let me come out of it."

John began to panic. He wondered if the Lord was going to help him like he had done many times before.

John then *imagined* hearing a voice say to him in a command-ing tone of voice as if he was being chewed out, *John, if I had allowed you to see me, I wouldn't have allowed you to return. Stay down there where you belong. It's not your time.*

After hearing that, John believed he had finally learned his lesson. He knew he had gone too far.

Having that being said and as John's vision continued, he remembered when the commissioner sent a new director to SYC. It was said through the grapevine that the new director was being sent to terminate people. John believed he was number one on his hit list.

The new director's name was Slaughter. Imagine that. He reminded John of the slave master in the movie *Uncle Tom's Cabin.* He was a short stubby fat man. It seemed like he had the arms and hands of a *Tyrannosaurus rex.*

John remembered one evening when he came to work early. He was in the lobby area. The lobby area was where the staff would check in before being assigned to their perspective dormitories.

Director Slaughter entered the lobby area, and a shift leader, who just so happened to be a Black man, was sitting down behind a desk. When the shift leader saw Director Slaughter, he jumped up as if he had seen a ghost.

"How are you doing, sir? It's a fine day, isn't it?" the Uncle Tom said.

"I'm doing great. I want you to make sure you do this right, and when you are done, report back to me," Director Slaughter said that to him in a demeaning tone of voice.

John believed the director was actually trying to show him he was in charge. He was talking to the shift leader as he periodically glanced at him.

John didn't know at the time whether or not the director knew who he was. He hadn't spoken to him since he became the director.

As John thought about that, he believed the director knew exactly who he was.

As fate would have it and as time passed, a local popular television show did a special on crimes committed by juveniles. John sent a copy of his research paper to the producer of that show.

It didn't take long. John received a response from the producer. The program was called *The Silhouette Show.* The producer asked him to be a guest on the show. John responded by saying that it would be an honor.

Having that being said, an ex-student of John had contacted him. He expressed his appreciation for what John had done for him.

John took that as an opportunity to see if the ex-student would appear on television with him.

John asked him if he would, and he said, "It would be an honor, Mr. Robinson. I'm glad you asked me."

As fate would have it, the ex-student and John appeared on *The Silhouette Show*. Everything went just right. The producer and his staff enjoyed it. John was told that the show was taped, and it would be aired in thirty days.

John knew there was going to be some mad people on his job once they found out what he had done.

Having that being said, and as time passed, the thirty days had gone by. The show was going to be aired on a Sunday.

John decided to use a vacation day to take off from work on that Sunday. He wanted to be able to watch the show in peace.

John watched the show. He was impressed with his performance, and as fate would have it, a fellow coworker came to his house after the show had aired.

"Man, I got something to tell you. They are mad at you. They didn't appreciate you being on television. I heard as soon as you come back to work, they are going to fire you," the coworker said.

"I appreciate the heads up," John replied.

As fate would have it, several months prior to John being seen on television, a representative from the Department of Corrections came to SYC to talk about stress in the workplace. It was said that stress was an illness.

John decided to see if they were really concerned about stress in the workplace. He had never been off from work more than two days on sick leave before.

He wouldn't have needed a doctor's excuse if he decided to take off from work for two days using his sick leave. He would have needed a doctor's excuse if he had taken off sick for three days in a row and/or if he had a history of taken off from work using sick leave.

The following Monday, after he had been seen on television, he went to see a doctor who just so happened to be a psychiatrist.

He actually needed some time to think of a strategy and to come up with a game plan to combat whatever decision the administration had set for him.

John complained about the stress he had been going through on his job as well as what he was going through at home. He really was telling the truth.

He knew how dangerous it was for him to go see a psychiatrist. He knew the administration would try to say he wasn't mentally fit to perform his duties.

His intention was to take off from work for three days using sick leave, not including the one vacation day he had already taken off from work to watch that show.

He really wasn't in a hurry to go back to work anyway. He knew the demons at SYC were biting at the bit to see him.

"Doctor, I have been going through a lot of stress on my job. I believe I have become a target. It seemed like several administrative officials are watching me and waiting for me to make a mistake. I also have been going through some rough times at home," John said in a low tone of voice.

John thought about what he had said to the psychiatrist. He said to himself, *Well, I'm committed now. If I didn't know any better, if I was the psychiatrist, I probably would have thought that I need some psychological help too, especially after hearing what I had just said. I know now I have got to be careful.*

The doctor gave John some medication to take and he listed John as an outgoing patient. He had given John ten working days to be off from work.

That's more than what I had expected, John said to himself with a smile on his face. He took advantage of it.

Having that being said, on the eleventh working day on a Monday, John returned back to work. He assumed that the administrators couldn't wait to see him. He thought they would be waiting for him at the front door.

John acted as if nothing was wrong. He submitted his doctor's excuse to his immediate supervisor, and he performed his normal duties.

Having that being said, several days had passed, and no one had said anything to John about being on television and/or about his doctor's excuse.

As fate would have it, the director eventually had his assistant to do his dirty work. His assistant's name was Willie. John called him Spiderman.

Spiderman was a Black man. He, in John's opinion, was a yes man as well as an Uncle Tom. He had been trying to find a reason to suspend John for quite some time.

John remembered on many occasions seeing Spiderman creeping alongside the walls in the hallway that led to his dormitory. He observed him peeking through windows and hiding behind doors.

Spiderman had an assistant named Sam. In a way, Sam was just like Spiderman. John called him Spider Boy. He was a student at the Nashville School of Law, and he was very proud of himself.

Actually, John really couldn't blame him for that. However, Spider Boy thought he was smarter and better than John because of the position he held.

It came to pass. Spider Boy said, "Robinson, Willie needs to see you in his office."

John remembered walking into Spiderman's office. Spider Boy was hot on John's trail. He must have thought John was going to run away or something.

Spiderman was sitting at his desk. He had a smile on his face when John walked into his office. John could have sworn he had seen horns protruding through Spiderman's skull.

"Robinson, we are going to suspend you for ten days for violating the Sick Leave Policy. You have the right to appeal our decision," Spiderman said.

John was glad that he was a rational-thinking man. He wanted to smack that grin off of Spiderman's face.

Having that being said, they had carried out their decision. John was suspended for ten days.

Damn! The way this is going, I'll probably have a month of being off from work under my belt before this is all over with, John said to himself.

John believed they expected that he would appeal their decision about being suspended. What they didn't expect was that he would file a grievance on each one of them for retaliation.

His plan was to kill two birds with one stone. He knew they were wrong and he was right.

John remembered the day he returned back to work. He noticed those demons looking at him as if they had done something very clever. They smiled when they looked at John.

As fate would have it, and as time passed, a representative from the State Department finally arrived at SYC to oversee the appeal and grievance hearing. The representative was a female. Her name was McGee.

John was told to sit outside the hearing room until he was called to testify. John represented himself.

It just so happened, prior to entering the hearing room, John could hear the director, Ms. McGee, Spiderman, Spider Boy, and a few other people talking and laughing. It appeared to him that they were having a good time.

Having that being said, and unknowing to them, when John entered the hearing room, he had a tape recorder in his hand. The tape recorder was behind his back.

They all were still engaged in their conversations as if he wasn't there until he eased the tape recorder from behind his back to his front so that they could see it.

The talking and laughter came to an abrupt halt. One could hear a pin drop, just like that. John smiled, and it took everything he had within his power to keep from bursting out laughing when he had seen the expressions on their face.

"Now that Mr. Robinson is here, let us get started. How are you doing, Mr. Robinson?" Ms. McGee asked.

"Fine, and you," John replied.

"I'm fine, thank you," she said.

"Mr. Robinson," she said, "we are here today as a result of an appeal and grievance that you have file against your director and the department. I am here as a neutral party to make sure you get a fair hearing.

"You have been accused of violating the department's Sick Leave Policy, and you had been suspended for ten days without pay as a result of it. I want to hear your side of the story. Director Slaughter, please present your case."

"If you don't mine, I will let Sam read the Sick Leave Policy," he replied.

Spider Boy said, as if he had an open and shut case, "The Sick Leave Policy states that an employee must present a doctor's excuse upon taking three or more days off from work.

"Mr. Robinson failed to comply. He had taken off from work for a total of eleven working days. Therefore, he violated the Sick Leave Policy by taking off an additional day instead of the ten days that he was given permission to take off by his doctor."

Spider Boy, in John's opinion, was acting as if he was in a court of law. He must have thought he was Perry Mason. Perry Mason was the character and a lawyer on the *Perry Mason Television Show*.

Having that being said, John remembered seeing himself praying and taking a deep breath before he responded. His integrity was on the line.

"First of all, I appreciate you for being here, and I respect your position," John said to Ms. McGee. "I didn't violate the department's Sick Leave Policy. According to my attendance record as far as taking time off from work is concerned, you can plainly see that I had never taken off sick from work more than three days before.

"They have accused me and suspended me for violating the Sick Leave Policy. They are wrong. They were the ones that had violated policy as a result of what they have done to me.

"The doctor had given me an excuse to be off from work for ten days. I was off from work according to the legal authority of my doctor. I had utilized an authorized vacation day for the day that I had taken off from work on that Sunday. I didn't need a doctor's excuse for that day," John said to Ms. McGee in a professional manner.

Ms. McGee then said, in a tone of voice as if she was surprised, "Director Slaughter, weren't you aware of that? Mr. Robinson has a valid point. If that is this case, he is correct."

Having that being said, and to John's surprise, Director Slaughter apparently couldn't take it any longer. He jumped up from his chair and said to John in a loud tone of voice, "Robinson, if you were that sick, how is it that you appeared on television?"

At that instant, one could hear a pin drop on carpet. The director acted as if he had caught John in a trap. Spiderman and Spider Boy smiled. John could sense that they were eagerly and impatiently waiting on him to respond.

Having that being said, John remembered saying to himself, *So that is what this is all about. He's upset about me being on television. I already suspected that. He couldn't suspend me for being on television, so he suspended me for violating the department's Sick Leave Policy instead.*

John paused before giving a response. Everyone was still waiting on him to respond. It was like a cliff-hanger in a movie and/or a book. He took his time on purpose. He looked into everyone's eyes, one at a time. He knew they were expecting him to incriminate himself.

John smiled, and then he focused his attention on the director. He looked straight at him and said very calmly, "Mr. Slaughter, to answer your question, being on television was my way of relieving stress."

One could again hear a pin drop on carpet after John said that. It was as if time had stopped. There was nothing that none of them could say in their defense.

"Mr. Robinson, it has been a pleasure to meet you. A decision will be made, and you will be notified of my decision," Ms. McGee said.

As fate would have it, John's ten-day suspension was stricken from his personnel file, and his pay was restored back to him.

As a result, John's reputation for standing up against the department's wrongdoing had become known throughout the institution, the Department of Corrections, and at the state capitol.

John believed, as far as those demons were concerned, he had become "state enemy number one."

Having that being said, the administrators of SYC continued to put pressure on John. It had gotten to the point where he knew he couldn't do anything wrong. They were waiting like vultures with a napkin around their necks and a fork in their hands.

He began to wonder what was more important to him, work or school. He needed to pass two algebra courses in order to graduate from college. He was weak in those subjects. He needed to take an intermediate algebra course prior to taking the two Algebra Courses 101 and 102.

The problem that John had was the fact that the intermediate algebra course could only be taken at a certain time, and that time would have interfered with his work schedule. It would have caused him to be late going to work.

He knew by being late going to work, he would be giving those demons a perfect opportunity to terminate him for being late for work.

Having that being said, John decided his education was more important to him at the time. He decided to submit his resignation. He also tried to give himself a way out and enough time to change his mind in the event that his school schedule could be changed.

John submitted his resignation to Spider Boy by saying, "It is my intention to resign in two weeks as a result of a conflict that I am having in continuing my education and my employment schedule."

He didn't say he was actually going to resign at that time. He said he intended to resign on a certain date. That should have been his way out or so he thought.

Having that being said, two days after John had submitted his intention to resign letter, he was able to resolve the conflict that he had. John's school schedule was changed.

As fate would have it, John said to Spider Boy, "If you don't mind, I would like to rescind my intention letter of resignation. I have gotten my school schedule change, and there will no longer be a conflict with my work schedule."

Spider Boy said with a smile on his face that he would inform Willie.

Having that being said, the next day, Spider Boy said to John, "I had talked to Willie about your request. We're not going to do that. As far as we are concern, you will no longer be employed by us very soon."

As fate would have it, John remembered saying, *Damn! They finally got me. I can't financially fight them in court.*

In the meantime, Spider Boy, Jack, and a few other demons were telling the other employees that John would never be rehired. They all laughed about it.

As fate would have it and as time passed, John's time was up. His last night as a supervisor had come. He knew it was going to be a rough night for him.

As John remembered that night in his vision, a tear rolled down his face. He remembered standing before his students. One could hear a pin drop. He could see the tears in just about all of his students' eyes. It almost made him cry in front of them.

John did everything he could to prevent tears from forming in his own eyes. He walked to the back area of his dormitory as if he was looking for something. He was choked up. He had to wipe the tears from his eyes.

He came back and said, "I want every one of you to remember what I have tried to teach you. In life, every one of you someday will find yourself having to make a decision that will ultimately affect your life. A decision has been made that will now affect my life. I have tried to teach you how to survive in the real world. If you can just remember to follow the rules, regulations, policies, procedures, and the law, you'll be okay.

"And most importantly, you have to have faith in the Lord and believe in yourself. I want you all to know that I love every one of you as if you were my own children. Good night gentleman!"

Having that being said, John left his dormitory. It took him awhile to get to his car. As he sat in his car, he thought about his life and what he was going to do next.

He said, "Lord, I don't know what my future will bring, but one thing I do know is that I still have faith in you."

Then tears began to flow from his eyes. He cried.

As fate would have it, and to make matters worse, his wife had filed for a divorce. John didn't contest it. The fight was out of him. He figured in the long run it was going to be her lost and not his.

John let his ex-wife keep everything except one of his cars and his stereo system. He left everything else for his kids.

He rented a two-bedroom apartment that was located near the college that he attended, and it wasn't too far from where he had worked.

He had to start all over. It took him about two months to finally get everything that he needed to furnish his apartment. He really wasn't used to being by himself. He felt somewhat out of place.

Having that being said, he knew he had to survive, not only for himself but for his kids.

As fate would have it, John had a friend named Wayne. Wayne had already received his walking papers a few months before John received his. Wayne had two little girls. John asked Wayne if he wanted to be his roommate. Wayne happily accepted his offer.

Having that being said, Wayne was a waiter at the Hungry Fisherman Restaurant, and as fate would have it, three months prior to John's last day at SYC, Wayne was instrumental in helping John get a part-time job there. He worked as a waiter, and Wayne was the one that taught him.

John actually had earned a decent income as being a part-time waiter.

Having that being said, it was never his plan to become a full-time waiter. He had come to the conclusion that he, at least, had a place to work.

As John thought about that, he believed the Lord had provided him a way to continue to survive. He believed the Lord knew what was going to happen to him in advance. The Lord had prepared a way out for John.

It just so happened, those demons at SYC weren't aware that John had been working at the restaurant.

Having that being said, during the first month of John's employment as a full-time waiter, the demons at SYC had discovered where he was working, and they specifically would ask for him to be their waiter when they came there to eat.

They made fun of him. They tried to make him feel bad, and once they were finished eating, they would always leave loose change as their tip. Their change never did add up to being a dollar.

In spite of the way they treated him, John treated them professionally as he would any other patron.

As time passed, four months had passed. It was summertime. The thought of where John had been and what he lost, had gotten the best of him. He felt like he was going backward in life instead of forward.

Having that being said, he decided to take the intermediate algebra course again. The course was being taught in the county where his daughter had gone to college. In fact, it was the same college.

As fate would have it, John had to pass by the county Sheriff Department on his way to school.

Having that being said, one day, a familiar sensation came upon John. He *imagined* hearing a voice telling him to go to the Sheriff Department and fill out an application.

John had learned from past experiences to follow his instinct. He knew the Lord would be involved.

It just so happened there was a Black deputy sheriff who had recently been promoted to being the counties first Black detective. His name was Mark.

There were only three Black deputy sheriffs at the time. The sheriff had promoted Mark, knowing all along that he was only going to be there for two weeks as a result of him being hired by state's bureau of investigation.

As fate would have it, when John walked into the Sheriff Department, he was at the right place, right time, and probably the right color. He was hired on the spot. He became the third Black deputy sheriff. There was a big smile that came upon his face. He could hardly wait to tell Wayne.

Having that being said, he found an apartment to live in almost immediately. The apartment complex was new, and his apartment had never been occupied. The apartment complex was only fifteen minutes away from the college.

BOOK SEVEN

Deputy John D. Robinson

I n John's vision, he remembered the first day he reported to work. He had become the topic of conversation within the department whether he wanted to be or not. The word had spread throughout the department that he was hired.

There were individuals within the Sheriff Department who didn't like John right off the bat, and John hadn't met them yet.

It was unusual for an unknown, like John, to have basically walked in from off the street to be immediately hired as a deputy sheriff. If anything, a person would have had known someone with political connections outside the Sheriff Department as well as within the Sheriff Department to be hired.

Not only that, one would have had to start by working in the jail as a correctional officer before being a patrol officer. John was assigned to patrol. That meant he was going to be commissioned to carry a gun and issued a patrol car.

Having that being said, everything seemed to be going great for John for a change. The thought of knowing that he was the first one to occupy his apartment made him smile, and he felt good being back in law enforcement. The only two things that were missing in his life were his kids.

John remembered being introduced to his supervisor as well as the other deputies and employees that were there at the time. He spent the entire morning shift being issued his gear and uniforms. He was told that he would be assigned to the evening shift, which was 3:00 p.m. to 11:00 p.m.

John remembered his first night as being a deputy. He was in bed at the time. He thought about his life again. He was ready to perform his duties as a deputy sheriff. He was back in action.

In the meantime, Wayne and his ex-wife had gotten back together. John was happy for him.

John reported to work the next day on the evening shift. He was assigned to ride with Deputy Davenport. Deputy Davenport treated him with respect. He offered to loan John some money to get by on until he was paid. He didn't have to do that. John knew then that he was a good man.

In the meantime, John met the other two Black deputies. Ron and William were their names. William worked on the midnight shift, and Ron worked on the evening shift with John.

As time passed, John had to ride with another deputy after being trained by Davenport. His name was Freeman. Freeman was a lot younger than Davenport and John.

John actually had fun being Freeman's partner. They had solved quite a few criminal cases together. They were given a nickname. They were called Batman and Robin.

In the meantime, Ron and John had become friends. He was the only one within the department that John associated with on and off duty at the time.

Ron was one of those individuals who knew just about everyone in town. He knew the good things as well as the bad things about the majority of them, including the local officials and other law enforcement officers.

John didn't want to give the other deputies the impression that he was like Ron. John was hoping that he wouldn't be put in a situation where he would have to put them in their place if they tried to treat him the same way they have been treating Ron.

Having that being said, as time passed, the other deputies began to notice that Ron had begun to change. He was trying to project a professional image like John. He stopped letting the others pick on him. John was beginning to become proud of him.

As fate would have it, John was told by his supervisor that Ron was going to train him during the last week of his training. That didn't surprise John. Somehow, he knew that was going to happen.

It just so happened, prior to being assigned to ride with Ron, he and John had planned to celebrate John's last day of training by going out to a local club, which would have been on a Friday night. John had been anticipating and looking forward to going out that night, especially since he was a single man.

Having that being said, on the last night of training, just before Ron and John were scheduled to get off from work, Ron received a dispatch advising him that he needed to go and get his son from a local hotel and that his son was in room 312.

It just so happened John had met Ron's family. His son was only five years old.

"Ron, what's going on?" John said.

"I don't know," Ron replied.

They rushed over to the hotel. Ron knocked on the door as John stood on the side of the door with his weapon out by his leg. He didn't want to take any chances.

A young White adult female came to the door, and that was when Ron said, "Hey, Robinson, everything is okay. You can put your weapon away."

He and John walked inside after John had placed his weapon back in its holster.

"How are you doing, Ron," the female said.

"I'm fine," Ron said.

John still didn't know what was going on. He kept quiet and observed everything that was going on in that room.

John noticed that there was another young White adult female and an older White female in the room as well. It was apparent to John that Ron knew them.

John then figured out the reasoning behind the dispatch that Ron had received. John believed that was the female's way of getting him over to the hotel.

Having that being said, the older female who appeared to have been in her late fifties was sitting on a bed. She said to Ron, "I love you. If you leave me, I'm going to tell the sheriff."

After hearing that, John said to himself, *What have Ron gotten me into?*

John knew trouble was going to head his way sooner or later.

Ron grabbed the woman by her arm and led her to the bathroom. John could hear them arguing and the woman pleading with him and begging him not to leave her.

They then came out of the bathroom, and that was when he and John left.

As fate would have it, their supervisor was sitting in his patrol car when they came out of the hotel room.

John thought about that. He was so glad those females didn't follow them out of the hotel room. John could only image what his supervisor would have thought.

Maybe that was exactly what he was expecting, John thought to himself.

"Is everything all right?" John's supervisor asked.

"Yes, sir," John replied.

John knew that it wasn't over. Ron and John returned back to the Sheriff Department. They got off from work, and they went to a night club.

As time passed, everything seemed to be going pretty good for John. He hadn't heard anything else about the incident that had taken place at the hotel, and he was enjoying his position. He was having fun.

As fate would have it, one night while he was on patrol, he drove onto a vacant parking lot in a rural area. It was very dark. There weren't any light poles in that area.

Normally, he wouldn't have done that. There would have had been some type of light visible for him to feel comfortable.

As John sat there, he began to think about his life and how blessed he was and how he had come from being a waiter and back to being in law enforcement again.

Being a deputy is not like being a state trooper. At least I'm doing something that I enjoy doing, John said to himself.

Having that being said, a familiar sensation came over John. For some reason he had the urge to urinate. He got out of his patrol car, and he looked around to see if he was alone and to see if he couldn't be seen.

As John urinated on the ground, he felt strange. He, for some reason, became weak. It was like he was being cleansed and/or drained.

He then noticed what looked like to be a cross in the sky. That was when he realized that he was near a church. He believed the moonlight had somehow illuminated the cross that was on the steeple of the church, and it somehow reflected an image of a cross in the sky. He wondered what that was all about. He went back on patrol, thinking about it.

Having that being said, while on patrol, he noticed a car that appeared to have been following him. He didn't know for sure. For some reason, he felt that it was an unmarked patrol car.

John then headed toward a storage area as if he was conducting a security check of the property. He noticed that the driver of the car that he thought was following him had turned off the headlights and had stopped in the middle of the road. John knew then that he was being followed.

Having that being said, John still didn't know whether or not the vehicle was a patrol car.

He then headed toward his favorite hiding spot at a high rate of speed. His hiding spot was on top of a hill, and he could easily position his patrol car to where no one could see him. He could see traffic going away from him and coming toward him.

John managed to position his patrol car in enough time to prevent the driver of the vehicle that was following him from discovering his location, and sure enough, he saw that vehicle speeding down the road away from his location. Then all of a sudden, he saw that same vehicle make a U-turn and then passed his location at higher rate of speed.

John drove down from his hiding spot and pursued after the vehicle.

"Car 40 to dispatch," John said.

"Go ahead," the dispatcher responded.

"I'm in pursuit of a speeding vehicle," John said.

"We are sending units your way," the dispatcher responded.

"10-4," John said.

The driver of the speeding vehicle drove into a neighborhood in attempt to hide from John. John knew then that the vehicle that he was chasing was in fact an unmarked patrol car.

Having that being said, John felt the situation could get out of hand. He didn't want to be responsible for anyone getting hurt.

"Car 40 to dispatch," John said.

"Go ahead," the dispatcher responded.

"I've lost contact of that vehicle. You can call off the other units," John said.

"10-4," the dispatcher replied.

Actually, John didn't really lose contact with that vehicle. He hid behind a grocery store that was off the highway across from the neighborhood where the unmarked patrol car had gone.

John knew there were only one way in and only one way out of that neighborhood. John knew it would only be a matter of time before the driver of that unmarked patrol car to come out. He knew the driver couldn't stay in that neighborhood all night.

Having that being said, John saw the unmarked patrol car easing out from the neighborhood, just like a rat.

John waited, and sure enough, the unmarked patrol car got back onto the highway. John got behind it again, and he followed it at a high rate of speed. He didn't call it in, and he didn't activate his emergency equipment.

"Car 40 to dispatch," John said.

"Go ahead car 40," the dispatcher responded.

"Make contact with my supervisor and have him to meet me at the office," John said.

"10-4," the dispatcher responded.

John headed toward the Sheriff Department, and as soon as he entered the building, he saw the detective that was following him. He also had arrived. The detective lowered his head as he walked by John.

John could only *imagine* how stupid that detective felt in knowing that he had outsmarted him.

John told his supervisor what had taken place, and as a result, John was then placed on the day shift.

Having that being said, as time passed, John began to enjoy working on the day shift. He was able to get a lot of things done. He remembered an administrative sergeant had talked to him about getting involved in the Amway Business. They were supposed to meet at John's apartment on a certain day. Ron was also invited to come.

Having that being said, one day, two detectives arrived at John's apartment. Neither one of them were the ones that had followed him.

John thought they were coming to ask him if he wanted to join their Drug Task Force Unit.

"Robinson, we want to talk to you about what took place at the hotel," one detective said.

Here we go! I knew this day was going to come, John said to himself.

"We don't want you. We want Ron," the detective said.

"I don't know anything about it other than being dispatched to the hotel," John said.

They weren't pleased with John's response. He apparently didn't tell them what they wanted to hear. He could tell by the expression on their face when they left.

It just so happened, a few days later, the administrative sergeant that had asked John to get involved with him in the Amway Business showed up at his apartment. Ron didn't show up. John then called him.

"Hey, Ron, we are waiting on you. You did what? When did you do that?" John said surprisingly.

"Sergeant," John said, "Ron will not be coming. He just resigned along with two other deputies."

As fate would have it, several weeks had passed since Ron had resigned. John was told to report to Captain Brown's office.

"Robinson, we want to talk to you about a shoplifting conviction that you had in 1973," Captain Brown said.

"What shoplifting conviction?" John said.

Captain Brown showed John an FBI printout sheet that showed that he had been convicted of shoplifting. The captain said John had falsified his application by saying he never was convicted of a felony.

John was shocked and surprised. He was given the opportunity to be fired and/or to resign.

BOOK EIGHT

History in the Making

I n John's vision, he remembered when he went home that day. He laid across his bed as tears began to form in his eyes. He didn't know what he was going to do. He called several local lawyers and asked them if there was anything that they could do to help him. They all said there was nothing that he or they could do to help him being that the conviction was dated more than eleven years ago at that time.

They said even if they could help him, it would be very expensive, and there wouldn't be a guarantee that he would win.

Having that being said, John felt like his life and career in law enforcement was over. He had a criminal record and a conviction that he knew nothing about.

He had been a law enforcement officer long enough to know that just because a person was arrested, that didn't mean that person was convicted.

John knew in order for a person to be convicted of a crime and/or an offense, it would have had to take place in a court of law. He hadn't been in a court of law as a result of the shoplifting charge that he was convicted of.

Having that being said, John started to think back. He remembered in 1973, he had come home on a military leave. He was glad to be home. He went to visit his friend Ray.

John asked Ray if he would go to the Kmart Shopping Center with him. John wanted to buy an eight-track tape. Ray said that he didn't mind.

While in the store, Ray and John had gone in different directions. John was looking at several eight-track tapes. He selected the one that he wanted, and then he got in line to pay for it.

Having that being said, that was when he saw two men with their hands on Ray's shoulder. They were leading him to a room that was in the back of the store where John was. John got out of the line and went to the area where they had taken Ray.

"Excuse me! My name is John D. Robinson. I am home on military leave, and he is my friend. What's going on?" John inquired.

"Your friend was shoplifting, and we had called the police," they said.

As fate would have it, two metro policemen arrived on the scene. John could tell by their demeanor that they were racist. They had that look, and they had a negative attitude. John knew they had already made up their mind to arrest him too, especially when the security guards said that John was with Ray and seeing that John had the eight-track tape in his hand.

John was expecting the security guards to tell the officers that it wasn't him that was shoplifting. They didn't say a word.

One officer grabbed hold of John's arm. John attempted to tell the officer that it wasn't him that was shoplifting. The security guards still didn't say anything, and John believed the officers probably wouldn't have cared.

John didn't resist. He didn't want to give the officers a real reason to arrest him. John knew he was going to file a lawsuit against Kmart and the Metropolitan Police Department.

Having that being said, it just so happened during those days the military had assigned a military policeman to the county jails in the event an MP was needed for military personnel that were arrested. John knew the MP that was there at the time.

John had a brief opportunity to tell him what had happened. The MP said for John not to worry and that he was going to make sure he was taken care of.

John was placed in a holding cell, and he was told that he could obtain his release by paying a cash bond of $62.50. John contacted his mother, and she came to pay the bond for him.

"When will I be notified to come to court?" John asked the officers.

"Don't worry about it, boy. You will be notified," one officer said hatefully.

Having that being said, and as time passed, John's military leave had come to an end. He had to report back to his duty station.

John still hadn't heard a word from anyone about him being arrested, and he hadn't been given a court date.

Having that being said, John had often wondered what had happened to his case, and as time passed, he didn't think about it anymore. He had other issues going on at the time.

John remembered when he was hired at SYC. He knew there was going to be an investigation into his background. He thought if there was any record of him being convicted of a crime, he would have been told then.

Having that being said, nothing was ever mentioned to him about a shoplifting conviction, and again he didn't worry about it anymore. He went on with his career.

John thought about what his captain said to him. The captain said he had falsified his application.

John remembered there was a question on his application that asked if he had ever been convicted and arrested of a felony. John replied by putting a check mark in the box that said no.

When John realized that, he went back to the Sheriff Department, and he said to the sheriff, "The shoplifting charge that I was convicted of wasn't a felony. It was a misdemeanor. Therefore, I didn't falsify my application."

The sheriff looked at John as if he didn't care. He said, "It doesn't matter. I won't rehire you."

Having that being said, John returned back home, and he laid in his bed again. He thought about the time when he was hired. He knew there was a background check on him then, but nothing was ever said to him about a shoplifting conviction.

John prayed and said, "Lord, I don't know what I am going to do. The one thing that I do know is that I love you, and I know that you are with me. I know there has to be a reason for this. There must have been a reason why this incident had been kept dormant and me not knowing I was convicted of shoplifting. There have been too many agencies conducting background checks on me for this not to have been brought to my attention sooner."

Having that being said, the following morning, John headed back to Nashville. He had to swallow his pride. He tried to think positive. He went to see Wayne. He told Wayne what had happened. Wayne still worked at the restaurant.

As fate would have it, John was rehired at the restaurant. He became a full-time waiter again.

Having that being said, one week after he started back to work at the restaurant, a Metropolitan Police detective came on his job.

John had purchased a Chevrolet Camaro. The vehicle was a stolen vehicle the detective said. The dealership had purchased a stolen vehicle and had sold it to John.

"I know you didn't have anything to do with that. However, I have to confiscate your vehicle," the detective said.

The incident reminded John of the story he had read in his King James Version of the Bible. The story was "Job."

John lost his job as a deputy, he didn't have his kids, he didn't have a vehicle, and he still lived in the Rutherford County.

After John thought about that, there was a positive thing that had happened. He was glad that his kids weren't with him. That was a blessing he thought. He would have hated to put his kids in that situation to know what their father was going through.

Having that being said, Wayne drove John back home, and he took John to the dealership that sold him that car. The dealer let John get another vehicle.

Having that being said, as time passed and as fate would have it, John moved in with a coworker who lived in Nashville. The arrangement worked well for John.

Having that being said, as time passed, and after John had settled down, he began to focus on the shoplifting conviction he was accused of.

It just so happened one day he was reading a newspaper, there was a public defender lawyer named William. He was representing a person whose case had gotten John's attention.

It just so happened a week or so later, William had started his own law firm. That was when John decided to talk him.

John remembered the day he arrived at William's office.

William's secretary said, "Mr. Robinson, please have a seat in the lobby. William will see you in a few minutes."

John was nervous. He was thinking about his past experiences when no one would or could help him. He was also excited. He had a feeling that William was going to help him. He just didn't know for sure.

William's secretary led John to William's office. He was sitting down at his desk. He stood up and shook John's hand and said, "I'm William. What can I do for you?"

At that moment, John thought he could see a glow about William. It was as if there was an Angel of the Lord hovering over him. John then proceeded to tell him what had happened.

As fate would have it, William looked, smiled at John, and said, "John, I will help you. Write me out a check for the amount of $500. I will be getting back in touch with you," he said.

John smiled, and he said to himself, *After all I have been through, I know the Lord had sent me to him.*

There was no doubt in John's mind. He knew the Lord was with him.

In the meantime, John felt great. He knew sooner or later he was going to find out what had actually happened.

Having that being said, several months had gone by. William had finally contacted John and said, "John, I found the original warrant in the archive. You were arrested on December 21, 1973, and convicted on December 23, 1973, of a misdemeanor shoplifting charge.

"I now understand why you didn't know and why you weren't notified. You were denied the opportunity to contest the charge. You were denied due process of the law. I will file the proper papers, and I will get back with you."

Having that being said, no one at that time had ever brought back a misdemeanor shoplifting case to court before, especially at that time being thirteen years later.

As fate would have it, after all those years, John's attorney was able to get the old shoplifting case back into court. John's case had set a precedent. He was granted a new court date and a trial.

In the meantime, William and John had become friends. William became a candidate to run for a legislative position at the state capitol. John helped him on his campaign. John was also invited to William's wedding. John felt somewhat important being William's friend and him being his lawyer.

As time passed, John's court date had finally arrived. He was ready to testify.

"Everything is going to be okay, John. Don't worry," William said.

John was still worried. His heart was beating fast. His future was on the line.

John heard people talking and saying, "How in the world did he do that? How did he get his case to court thirteen years later?" Some people had wished John the best of luck.

John remembered the look on the city district attorney's face when the attorney looked at him. John could tell that the attorney was upset. His name was Story. It seemed like everyone in the courtroom was waiting on John's case to be heard.

As fate would have it, John was asked to sit down in the witness chair. John was nervous. He tried not to show it.

John was sworn in, and after William had presented the opening argument, John was asked to give his testimony.

John took a deep breath, and he said, "I was still in the Military, and I had come home on a military leave.

"My friend Ray and I went to a Kmart Department Store. I told him that I was going to look for an eight-track tape. He told me that he would be right back.

"Then about ten minutes later, I saw two men escorting him to a room near the back of the store where I was at the time. I was in line preparing to purchase an eight-track tape.

"I got out of line and proceeded to where they had taken him, and upon entering the room, I introduced myself as being in the Military and said that Ray was a friend of mine.

"I noticed that they had taken several items out of his pockets. They had apparently called the police. The police officers arrived. That was when the security guards told them that Ray had shoplifted some of the store's merchandise. The security guards didn't tell the officers that I wasn't involved. They said I was with Ray.

"I could tell the officers were racist by the way they were acting and by the way they were looking at Ray and me. I knew since the security guards didn't tell them that I wasn't involved, they weren't going to listen to me.

"I knew they were expecting me to argue with them. I knew better. I kept quiet. I was going to file a lawsuit against Kmart and the Metropolitan Police Department. They arrested Ray and me.

"After I was booked in jail and given the opportunity to use the phone, I asked the officers for my court date. One officer replied by saying, 'Don't worry about a court date, boy. You'll be notified.'

"My mother arrived about an hour later. She was told to pay sixty-two dollars and fifty cents. She paid that amount, and I was able to leave.

"I again inquired about my court date, and again, I was told not to worry about it and that I would be notified.

"As time passed, and after my military leave had come to an end, I returned back to my duty station.

"Having that being said, during the following months, I still hadn't been notified of a court date, and as time passed, I had been honorably discharged from the Army. I returned back home.

"I was hired by the state. I was assigned to Spencer Youth Center, which was a juvenile correctional institution.

"There was an intensive background check on me before I was hired. I was hired, and nothing was said about me being convicted of a shoplifting charge.

"I was hired by the Sheriff Department, and there was an intensive background check on me, and again nothing was said about me being convicted of a shoplifting charge until ten months after I had been hired.

"Actually, I should really be thankful that I had found out that I was convicted of a shoplifting charge. It was a blessing in disguise. I would have hated to have found out when I was too old to have done anything about it."

The district attorney then said, "You knew that you were arrested, didn't you? Why didn't you check to see when you were to appear in court? Why did you decide to check on it now? Is it because you had lost your job? In any event, the Statute of Limitations has expired."

John responded by saying to the attorney, "I had just got through telling you what had happened. Either you forgot or you didn't have anything else to say.

"The Statute of Limitations, as far as the law is concerned, has never been satisfied in this case. I never was given the opportunity to come to court. I was denied that right. I was denied due process of the law. That is why I am here today."

The district attorney responded and said, in a hateful manner, "It isn't the responsibility of the court to hold your hand and make you come to court. It is no excuse to be ignorant of the law. Even if the court failed to notify you, it's your responsibility to find out for yourself. After all, if the court rules in your favor, it will be opening up Pandora's box."

Having that being said, John knew exactly what he meant by that. Then the judge leaned over toward John from his seat. He took off his glasses, and he stared at John.

John said to himself, *Damn! He's upset too.*

John could sense it. Then the judge said, "Son, what are you trying to do? Are you trying to destroy the whole criminal justice system?"

John believed his heart had stopped. He knew whatever the judge was about to say after saying what he had just said, his future and career were going to depend on it.

The judge went on to say, "I can't make a decision in your case right now. I am going to take your case under advisement."

After hearing that, John's mind had wondered endlessly into his future. He was thinking about what he was going to do in the meantime and how long he was going to be made to wait.

John tried to think positive by saying to himself, *Well, at least he didn't say no.*

John had been given some breathing room.

Having that being said, and as time passed, William won his election. He became a very popular state representative. He was nominated as being the house majority leader.

In the meantime, and as time passed, John was miserable. It was hard for him to be patient. He was labeled as a thief, and his life at the restaurant was stagnated.

John thought he was on the verge of having a nervous breakdown. He had to keep reminding himself of what he had read in the King James Version of the Bible.

He remembered reading somewhere in the Bible a scripture that said that the Lord wouldn't put on a person more than what one could handle. John believed that scripture had helped him maintain his sanity.

As time passed, John finally received a letter from William. He didn't open it immediately. He looked at the envelope as he paced back and forth, thinking about what he was about to read. His heart began to beat faster. His mind began to wonder about the possibility of reading bad news.

He finally said, "This is it. It's what I have been waiting for."

John opened the envelope, and he read, "Dear, Mr. Robinson, this court finds that you failed to contest the charge of shoplifting. Your request to expunge and to forfeit the charge of shoplifting is denied."

John couldn't believe it. After all that time, he was denied. With that letter in his hand and tears running down his face, he paced back and forth, thinking about what he was going to do. He cried out to the Lord and to God, and said, "I need both of your help!"

As fate would have it, a few days later, William called John and said, "John, the prosecutor had talked to me and had asked me if I thought that you would appeal the decision of the court.

"In response, I said that I thought you would. The prosecutor went on to say that the court would probably agree to expunge your record if you would be willing to release the Kmart Department Store, the Metropolitan Police Department, and the Sheriff Department of all liabilities."

John really didn't want to do that. He wanted them all to pay for the suffering that he had to go through.

John thought about it. He responded and said, "I would agree to release them all. I'm tired of fighting the system. I just want to get it all behind me."

William then said, "I'll get back with you in a few days."

Having that being said, a week or two later, John was told to report to William's office.

When John arrived, William wasn't there. His secretary had several documents ready for him to sign. The first document pertained to him releasing everyone of all damages and liabilities.

John read it, and it said, "Mr. Robinson is agreeing to acquit and forever discharge all of the parties thereof and to forever discharge all of the parties of any and all past, present, and future actions, cause of actions, including claims or suits arising out of or from the citation issued to him."

After reading that, John again thought about the pain and suffering that he had gone through. He was actually upset.

I'm not going to let them get away with that, John said to himself.

The second document pertained to the Metropolitan Legal Division of the Police Department. It said, "Mr. Robinson, you are to sign the General Release Form on the date mentioned below."

Having that being said, the day they wanted John to sign those documents was on a Friday. They were very clever. They had John to come to William's office on the very last day that he could file an appeal, which at that time he only had four hours to do so.

The second document also said, "If by chance that any of the parties thereof decided to change their minds, they could do so in the near future."

John believed if he signed those documents, they would change their minds the very next day, and there would be nothing that he could do about it. He didn't want to take that chance. In fact, he was afraid to take that chance.

The third document was the letter that William had written to the Kmart Department Store Legal Division.

He wrote, "I appreciate the attitude and attention that Kmart Department Store had in this matter. It is a pleasure to find a large company willing to take an interest in the small problem of this individual, who finds himself confronted with this increasingly complex world."

Having that being said, John's heart was broken. He couldn't believe William would say something like that about him. Of all the documents, John believed that was the one that affected him the most. He needed more time to think about it.

John was under a lot of pressure. He didn't know what to do. He asked William's secretary to make him several copies of the documents. He wanted to take them to another lawyer who was related to one of his friends. He didn't tell the secretary what he was planning on doing.

John said to the secretary, "I can't sign those documents at this time. I'll come back within an hour to sign them."

Having that being said, John went to see that lawyer. He was a Black lawyer.

As fate would have it, he wasn't in his office. John was a nervous wreck. He was pacing back and forth. He couldn't sit down. His heart was beating fast, and he thought he was going to have to leave before he had an opportunity to talk to him. Time was passing by, and it was getting closer to his deadline.

Having that being said, the lawyer finally came. John only had two hours to go. John quickly told him about his problem. He offered John his opinion and said, "You are caught up in this vicious system, and there is no guarantee of you being successful."

His advice didn't help John at all. John could have avoided that stress by not seeing him. John thanked him and said goodbye. John only had an hour and a half to go.

John was under so much pressure and stress. He thought he was going to have a heart attack. His mind and thoughts had him wired up. He didn't know what he was going to do.

John went back at William's office. William's law partner was waiting on him.

John said, "I need more time to think about this. I can't sign those documents. I want to appeal it."

At that point, William's partner called William on the phone, and that was when William asked to speak to John.

Man, I really don't want to speak to him. I know he is going to be upset, John said to himself.

William said, "John, I understand how you must feel. What do you want? Do you want justice? True justice is in heaven and not here on earth."

John really didn't want to disappoint William. He had done so much for him.

Having that being said, John still said that he wanted to appeal the decision of the court. William then told his partner to escort John to the courthouse and to file an appeal. John could tell in the tone of William's voice that he was disappointed in him.

William's law partner handed the appeal's clerk several documents, and after the clerk looked at those documents, the clerk said, "How in the world did you get this far? I have to call my supervisor."

The clerk then called her supervisor, and when her supervisor arrived, she said the same thing.

The supervisor processed the documents and said, "I don't know how you did it. Your case is hot. No wonder no one wanted to touch it."

After the supervisor said that, John began to wonder what she knew behind the scenes.

William's partner looked at John and smiled. John could sense that he was glad that he had filed an appeal. John believed he had winked at him as to say, "Good!"

Having that being said, when John returned home, he thought about what he had just gone through. He thought about William. He *imagined* the position he must have put him in.

At first, John was William's client, and then he became his friend. John *imagined* what William's peers must have said to him: *William, we realize that you are a good lawyer, and we believe that you believe in your client. However, you are one of us now. We are among a secret society. What goes on behind our closed doors are to be kept private among us. You have caused the possibility of our door being opened to the public. We cannot allow John to come in. His case has the potential to reveal what goes on inside of our house. If it is discovered, our way of doing things will be revealed and exposed.*

BOOK NINE

Innocent Only
Upon Proof

In John's vision, he remembered when he received the letter from the court of appeals. William and John were to appear in court on a certain date.

Having that being said, the day had come for them to appear in court.

A court of appeals judge said to John, "This court decided to put the appeal process on hold. This court felt that it hadn't given you a fair amount of time to look over the documents. This court will give you an additional thirty days to do so."

In the meantime, John had already made up his mind. He wasn't going to sign those documents. He didn't trust the government. He still thought they would change their mind after he would sign those documents. And John still wanted the option to file a lawsuit.

Having that being said, thirty days later, William and John had appeared in the court of appeals again. There were about five judges sitting together at a long table. They all were looking at John. He could only *imagine* what they were thinking. It was like they were saying to themselves, *Come on, son, let's get this over with.*

John knew they all were expecting him to sign those documents.

John said, very nervously, "I'm not going to sign those documents."

John believed they couldn't believe what they had just heard. John could tell by the expression on their face. John was asked to repeat what he had just said.

As fate would have it, William looked at John as he shook his head and said, "Your Honor, there appears to be a conflict in my client and attorney relationship. With your permission, I would like to be released from my obligation to represent Mr. Robinson."

The court granted William's request. John was given another thirty days to find another lawyer.

Having that being said, John left the building with tears in his eyes. The system had gotten him again.

John remembered while at home, he thought about what William said to him about justice.

John said to himself, *I once knew a man named William, who had once said that true justice was in heaven and not on earth.*

It took John a while to understand what William actually meant. He meant hell instead of the earth. John finally realized where he was and whom he was up against.

Having that being said, John felt that William had jumped the ship on him. He really wasn't mad at him for doing so. He understood the position that William was in. He really believed William was pressured by his peers to do what he had done.

Most importantly, John couldn't forget the fact that it was him who had helped him get as far as he had. Actually, John felt sorrier for him than himself.

Having that being said, as time passed, time was winding down for John. He hadn't been able to get anyone to represent him. In fact, he hadn't tried.

John remembered the tears that formed in his eyes and was running down his face. He prayed and said, "Lord, I don't know what else I can do. Tomorrow will be the last day that I can file an appeal, and I still don't have anyone to represent me. What am I going do?"

John then *imagined* hearing a voice say, *Call William and ask him to represent you, and tell him that you will sign those documents.*

John thought about what he *imagined* hearing *and* what he was told to do.

Why would he help me now? John said to himself.

As fate would have it, John did what he believed the Lord had instructed him to do. John called William and said, "William, I need your help. I will sign those documents."

"John, I will help you. Come to my office tomorrow," he said in a very understanding tone of voice.

Having that being said, the next day, John signed those documents. He didn't consider himself giving up. He did what he had to do.

As fate would have it, as time passed, John received a letter from the court of appeals. It was the letter he had been waiting for.

John remembered taking a deep breath as he opened the envelope. His mind was wondering about his future. The letter stated, "As a result of your being denied the right of trial, it is therefore ordered, by agreement, that the charge placed upon you, John D. Robinson, shall be dismissed and all public records expunged pursuant to law."

After John read the letter, tears began to roll down from his face.

He said, "Injustice! It's a crying shame. Many people are hurt, and there are many people to blame. Every one of us makes mistakes. But when the government makes a mistake, it doesn't accept the blame. Injustice! It's a crying shame."

Having that being said, John decided that it was best for him to move. He was able to rent a house, and it just so happen Wayne had received his walking papers again. As a result, Wayne became John's roommate again.

As time passed and as fate would have it, John received a check for the amount of $62.50 from the Metropolitan Court. It was the amount of money his mother had paid for him to get out of jail. That was apparently his compensation.

Having that being said, John tried to think positive. His case had set a precedent, and most importantly, his record had been expunged. He finally had closure.

As fate would have it, and as time passed, John met his present wife, who at the time became his girlfriend.

Having that being said, it seemed like to him that his life was getting back on track. He was able to get another job. He became a security guard.

Having that being said, being a security guard wasn't what he wanted to do, but it at least gave him a chance to work in the field of criminal justice again. He was assigned to work at the state museum.

As fate would have it, and as time passed, John was promoted to being an assistant supervisor, and it just so happened the Magna Carta, the Bill of Rights, and the United States Constitution was going to be held as an exhibit at the museum.

Having that being said, John remembered being asked by his superior if he wouldn't mind being interviewed by one of the local television stations. He was to be asked to give his opinion of how he felt about the exhibits that were coming to the state museum.

"I don't mind that at all. It would be an honor," John said with a smile upon his face.

His supervisor couldn't have asked a more perfect person. John couldn't wait to be interviewed.

As time passed, the television station arrived. The crew had set up the light fixtures and had set the cameras in place.

John was then asked the magic question: What does the Magna Carta, the Bill of Rights, and the Constitution of the United States mean to you?

As fate would have it, John felt a feeling of rejoice. He said, "You don't know how much it really means to me to be able to tell you how I feel about the Magna Carta, the Bill of Rights, and the Constitution of the United States of America.

"If it hadn't been for due process of the law and the Constitution of the United States of America, I wouldn't be working here today, and a lot of innocent people would have been at the mercy of the government. Believe me, I am living proof."

Having that being said, as time passed, John decided to go back to Spencer Youth Center in an attempt to get his old job back.

It just so happened Spider Boy had taken Spiderman's place, and Spiderman had been transferred downtown. Director Slaughter was promoted to being a warden over a prison.

It seemed like to John that everyone who had a hand in his departure had been promoted. It was apparent to John that the promotions were their reward.

John could tell by the way Spider Boy was acting that he thought he was still better than him. John's reputation was still known, and a lot of people wished him good luck in trying to come back.

"What are my chances of being rehired," John asked Spider Boy.

In a way, John hated having to ask him that.

"Mr. Robinson," he said in a sarcastic tone of voice, "I want to be completely honest with you."

In John's opinion, Spider Boy had lied already.

"Just because I know you don't mean that you will be rehired. You still have to fill out an application just like everyone else. Then, if we decide to hire someone, we will set up an interview committee. I'm sure that your background will weigh heavily in your favor. You probably wouldn't want the job anyway. You would have to start all over again, and you would start at the beginning salary, which isn't that much at all."

John said to himself, *You snake in the grass. You're trying your best to discourage me.*

Spider Boy made a point to let John know that his vote would be a major factor in determining who the director would hire.

Having that being said, John also knew if it was the Lord's will, Spider Boy wouldn't be able to stop him from being rehired.

Book Ten

Fate

As fate would have it, Spencer Youth Center was under the leadership of a new superintendent. His name was Henderlight.

It just so happened Mr. Henderlight was well aware of John's past. He needed someone with John's experience. John didn't know that at the time.

There was a unit that was called Programmatic Segregation Unit. It was a special unit that housed students that had major psychological and behavioral issues.

The administration had problems maintaining order in that unit, and it was hard to retain staff members once they had been assigned to work in that unit.

As a result, the Department of Human Services and the Department of Corrections's Legal Division had been monitoring that unit. It was the first of its kind for incarcerating those types of children.

As fate would have it, John was at the right place at the right time. Mr. Henderlight sent a memo to Spider Boy, stating that he wanted John rehired. John also wasn't aware of that fact until later on.

Having that being said, after all the things Spider Boy had said to discourage John, his tactic and plan didn't work.

Spider Boy had no other choice but to tell John that he had been rehired. John could tell that Spider Boy didn't want to tell him.

John also found out that no one else had been interviewed. There was no need to interview anyone else as far as John was concerned.

"I want to welcome you back. I am glad I had the opportunity to have had an input in you being rehired. It looks like you will not be starting over as if you were a first-time employee. You will been given a pay raise, and the sick leave time that you had left when you were here before will be restored to you," Spider Boy said.

John smiled, and he said to himself, *Being rehired worked out better than I thought.*

John was immediately assigned to the Programmatic Segregation Unit.

Having that being said, he had to attend a two-week training course at the State Department Correction Training Academy. That was something he hadn't had to do before.

In the meantime, John's younger brother had moved back to Nashville from Atlanta, Georgia. His name was Antonio. He had a two-bedroom apartment.

John decided to help his brother out by being his roommate, and he let Wayne take the responsibility of the house.

Having that being said, John remembered the first day back at SYC. He noticed that the rank structure had changed. It was based on the Military Ranking System.

John was assigned to the 3:00 p.m. to 11:00 p.m. shift. PSU was located away from the other dormitories. It was like a dungeon. It had an iron front door.

Normally, a new officer would have been assigned a training officer to work with during the first week at least. John only had a training officer for ten minutes, just long enough for him to be given the keys.

It looks like I will be starting from where I had left off, John remembered saying to himself.

John was the main officer in charge of PSU. There were about ten students in PSU at that time. John referred to them as being gifted. He looked at them, and he said to himself, *Damn! I believed I got my hands full this time. I believe this task isn't going to be easy.*

John gave them the same speech as he had done before in the past. He also said some things he hadn't said before. He threatened them.

John said, "I want you to know that I am not a rookie officer. I have worked here before. I am an ex-police officer, and I am a black belt in martial arts. I'm not afraid of you."

For some reason, John felt he had to get that point across to them.

Having that being said, John believed those monsters were the cream of the crop.

He was referring to his gifted students. He believed his students could be a person's worst nightmare, like in the movie *Nightmare on Elm Street*. They also reminded him of the kid that was on the television show called *The Munsters*. Each one of them had at least three different personalities, and it didn't take that much for them to turn into their true form that was Little Eddie Munster.

John believed they could tell that he wasn't like the rest of the officers that had worked there and whom they had devoured.

He decided to do something a little different with them. He wanted them to know that he cared about them. He wanted to find out how much human was left in them.

He said to them, "I want to give all of you an opportunity to tell me exactly what is on your mind and what is it that I can do for you."

John could tell he had caught them by surprise. The majority of them had a smile on their face when he said that.

John listened to their concerns and their complaints. Their main complaint was about the other officers and staff. John already knew it would be. They felt that their counselor didn't spend enough time with them and that he was lazy. His name was Tally.

They felt that the corporal, who was actually over John, spent more time taking care of church business than his job. He was a pastor. His name was Smith.

Having that being said, and as time passed, John realized that the majority of the things they had told him were true.

It didn't take long for John's students to figure him out. They realized that he was a serious person, and he didn't tolerate inappropriate behavior. They also found out that they couldn't manipulate him. Most importantly, they realized that he really did care for them.

It took a while for John to finally get things organized. It was something that the corporal should have done a long time ago. It took all the skills that John had to finally get control of them. It was like getting a child to sit down in a dentist chair of which he knew he would have had a problem doing himself.

As time passed, John again gained the reputation of being one of the best officers on campus. He had managed to prevent a lot of problems that had occurred in PSU before his arrival, and it was noticed by the Department of Youth Services Legal Department, the Department of Human Services, and Mr. Henderlight.

As time passed, Antonio had gotten another job, and he had to move back to Atlanta. As a result, John kept the apartment, and that was when his girlfriend moved in with him.

In the meantime, Mr. Henderlight and John had talked on many occasions. He said he was pleased with John's performance and what he had done for the institution.

John heard on several occasions Mr. Henderlight telling other members of his administration, including Spider Boy, that he was glad to have rehired him.

As time passed, John was finally off probation. Everything was going good for him for a change. He heard through the grapevine that there was going to be three corporal positions coming up. He was hoping that he would be promoted.

In the meantime, John had gotten back in school. He was able to take Algebra 101 and 102 back-to-back. He had failed the classes so many times before that he thought he knew enough about both classes to at least pass with a C.

Having that being said, John remembered one night when he was at home. He laid down on his bed, and he crossed his fingers together behind his head as he stared at the ceiling fan. He thought about his life and what he had been through. He prayed to the Lord and said, "Lord, thank you for being with me. You have been with me a long time."

As time passed, John thought about getting back in law enforcement. He had set his sights on becoming a state trooper. He thought it would be easier for him to become a trooper because he was already a state employee. He was already in the system.

Having that being said, in the meantime, Mr. Henderlight told John that he was going to promote him to the corporal position. He said John deserved it. He also expressed to John that he really didn't want him to leave PSU.

He also said that John still had to go through the interview process even though he knew he was going to be promoted.

As fate would have it, John received a phone call from Spider Boy.

He said, "Mr. Robinson, I was told if you were selected to be promoted, you would not be willing to transfer to another shift. I just wanted to make sure."

John remembered saying, "Someone must have given you the wrong information. I have no problem being transferred if I were to be promoted."

John believed Spider Boy was trying his best to find a reason for him not to be promoted.

Spider Boy then said, "Well, I just wanted to make sure. That's all."

Having that being said, Spider Boy had actually confirmed that John was about to be promoted.

As days went by, John decided to go to Spider Boy's office. His intention for doing so wasn't really good.

John stood in the doorway of Spider Boy's office. He had a grin on his face. He was ready for combat.

John said, "I just wanted to let you know that I appreciate everything that you have done for me."

Spider Boy then said, "Mr. Henderlight asked me who did I think ought to be promoted. I told him that I didn't know of anyone."

After hearing that, Spider Boy had made John mad.

John then said, "I'm pretty sure you'll think of someone."

John left Spider Boy's office mumbling. He should have known better. He knew he was the one that started it by trying to upset Spider Boy.

The responsibilities of a corporal consisted of being the leader of a given area. They were in charge of only one dormitory as well as being responsible for the other officers that worked within that dormitory.

As fate would have it, John was promoted to the corporal position. Mr. Henderlight personally assigned John's duties.

John was in charge of Pierce Dormitory. Pierce Dormitory was located next to the Control Unit. John was also in charge of PSU and the new Classification Unit. PSU and the Classification Unit were actually counted as two dormitories within the same building.

Having that being said, Corporal Smith was still assigned to PSU and also the new Classification Unit. The Classification Unit was where the new students were sent to. Those students were located in a separated area from PSU.

There were officers and high-ranking officers upset with John, especially the ones who had never left SYC when he was there the first time. They wanted someone within their social click to be promoted.

John believed Jack had something to do with that by stirring them up. John's sergeant and lieutenant were like two peas in a pod. They were in charge of the second shift.

John's lieutenant's name was Crutcher. John thought Crutcher would give him a chance to do his job. On the other hand, John's sergeant was like a weasel. His name was Pete. John didn't trust him at all.

As fate would have it, Jack was the senior corporal. He was in charge of the security detail on the second shift, and when the lieutenant and sergeant were off, he was in charge of the shift.

Having that being said, when Jack wasn't working, John was in charge of the security detail. John's days off was changed. He was off on Fridays and Saturdays, and he worked a split shift on Sunday. He had to work every other Sunday on the first shift and then on the second shift.

John was the second man in charge when he worked on the first shift. He liked that shift the best, and he liked the lieutenant on that shift. His name was Donahue.

It was the second shift that John found himself having problems. He was forced to work among the wolves in sheep's clothing. The advantage that he had was the fact that he knew those of whom were in the pack.

John remembered being instructed by Lieutenant Crutcher to observe Jack and Corporal Everett for a week. John was to learn how the security detail operated.

Corporal Everett only worked security on special occasions. His main responsibility was to be in charge of Crockett Dormitory. He was the type of person who enjoyed being in charge. He was also one of Jack's favorite followers. Jack would let him work on the security detail whenever he could.

Having that being said, for a brief time, Everett enjoyed being in the position to tell John what he thought John should do.

He said, "Robinson, I'm not trying to tell you what to do. It's just how we do things around here."

Then Jack said sarcastically and with a smirk on his face, "Look, son, you're like a new fish in the water. You can't just come back here and change the water."

John really wanted to tell Jack something else other than what he had eventually said to him.

John said, "Jack, I may be a new fish, but don't forget, I had swam before in that old nasty dirty water that you and the others are still in. Now, it is time to change it."

John could tell by the expression on their faces that they didn't like what he had said.

As time passed, John began to see why they didn't want him working with them. John was able to get things done the right way, and they also knew the superintendent liked him.

Having that being said, John then thought that his superiors might have thought that he wanted their positions. Actually, John hadn't thought about that.

He was locked up behind the walls of the dungeon in PSU as an officer. He couldn't see the evil and the corruption that was taking place by them.

John believed they felt that he was intruding on their stomping ground. They all had done things together that were against policy. There was a policy that prohibited an on-duty officer or corporal to directly participate in games with the students, except under special circumstances. The administrators felt that they couldn't supervise their students effectively if they were physically playing games with them.

It just so happened, on a few occasions, Jack, Pete, Crutcher, and John would walk together through the dormitories conducting a security check and to make sure everything was running smoothly.

John observed several officers and corporals playing pool with their students, and nothing was said or done about it.

When John walked through the dormitories by himself, things were a little different. They would drop their pool sticks and would walk away from the table as if they hadn't been playing pool.

As time passed, the conspirators tried to make John look bad. One night, Crutcher and Pete approached John.

Crutcher said, "Robinson, several people feel that you are taking your job too seriously and that you should slow down. Some of them have been here for quite some time. They resent you being in charge over them.

"However, you are not over them. You aren't over another corporal. You all have the same title and rank. I admit that you do have additional duties than the other corporals. We just want you to take it easy. Let them hang themselves."

John still liked Crutcher. He continued to give him the benefit of the doubt. John felt Crutcher had the potential of being a good leader. It was just that his closet was too dirty, and the grip that the others had on him was too strong for him to break loose.

As time passed, there were several dormitories outside on the playground. John was in charge of setting up the security perimeter.

Corporal Triplett just so happened to be working on the security detail that day with John. Triplett was also in charge of a dormitory. John instructed him to position himself near the basketball court.

It just so happened Triplett was one of those persons who John had caught playing pool with the students.

Triplett ignored John's instruction and walked away. He went to the command post, which was in the lobby.

When he returned, John tried to explain to him his reasoning for giving him the instruction. Triplett again refused to follow John's instructions.

"I'm not going to, and you can write me up if you want to," Triplett said very angrily.

John honored his request.

As time passed, John was informed that Triplett had filed a grievance against him. John read his complaint.

Triplett said, "Corporal Robinson had on several occasions, and for no apparent reason, approached me in a very negative way, which tends to cause job animosity.

"Corporal Robinson attempts to be very aggressive in demonstrating his rank toward me and the other staff. Also, he exhibits very little professionalism in his employee interactions. His behavior and personality disrupt a workable relationship and cause an employee's self-esteem to be infringed upon. Thus, I request that Corporal Robinson be reprimanded for his unbearable interactions with his fellow employees and, furthermore, that he no longer present a negative approach toward me and the other employees."

It seemed like to John that Triplett couldn't stand on his own. He had to add other officers as well. He was a coward as far as John was concerned.

Having that being said, to keep from having a grievance hearing and having the department's legal staff getting involved, Crutcher and Pete wanted to have a meeting with Triplett and John. John knew what he was up against.

They knew if a grievance hearing was to take place, John would have exposed every dirty thing that they all had been doing.

John really expected Crutcher to reprimand Triplett. But instead, he tried to smooth things out by saying, "Why don't you two shake hands and try to work things out?"

John shook his hand.

As time passed, John really began to feel the daggers of the conspirators. On several occasions when Crutcher wasn't working,

Sergeant Pete was left in charge. Pete would let Jack be in charge of all the assignments. He let Jack do his dirty work.

Jack took advantage of John by assigning him to work in one of his dormitories. That way, John would be out of their way.

Having that being said, according to policy, Jack had the authority to assign him to a dormitory in the event of an emergency and/or when there was a shortage of employees.

On those occasions, Jack would get Everett out of his dormitory, and he would assign an officer to work in Everett's place. Everett took John's place as for security, and John had to work in a dormitory that he was responsible for. That way, they, along with a few other conspirators, would be in charge of the entire campus.

They all took advantage of their authority. They tried to upset John by walking through his dormitory. They would laugh out loud and would cause a disruption in his dormitory.

Having that being said, John reported what had taken place to Crutcher. Crutcher and Pete assured John that it wouldn't happen again. They lied. The pressure was on John again, just like in the old days.

John remembered one night when he was lying down in bed, he began to think about his life again. It seemed like old times had returned. He was really frustrated. He started to complain to Mr. Henderlight. He decided to rely upon his faith in the Lord instead.

As fate would have it, John had gotten wind that the highway patrol had a position open within their Capitol Police Division. He submitted his application and résumé.

In the meantime, the Department of Corrections youth institutions were being downsized. That meant other officers from other juvenile institutions were going to be relocated. It also meant that those who had rank could use their seniority to bump those individuals with lesser seniority and rank.

John heard through the grapevine that there were going to be several ranking officers coming to SYC, which meant that it was possible that he, along with several other ranking officers, would be bumped back to their previous rank and positions.

The administrators had a meeting with all the staff that was going to be affected by the downsizing. John, along with a few others who had been recently promoted to the corporal position, was going to be bumped back to their previous rank and position.

As fate would have it, in John's case, Mr. Henderlight had informed him that he would be keeping his same duties and pay. The only thing that he was told he was going to lose was his title as a corporal.

As time passed, all hell broke loose. The fact that John wasn't a corporal had stirred up the demons. The conspirators came out of the woodwork after him in full force.

Pete, Triplett, Everett, Jack, and Spider Boy made it hard on John. It had gotten to the point where he didn't have anyone to turn too. They made sure that he wasn't able to work outside with them. And to make matters worse, Mr. Henderlight had been promoted, and he was in the process of being transferred to another location. That would have left John all alone.

John thought about the stories he had read in the King James Version of the Bible. He felt like Samson when his hair was cut. He felt like Jonah sitting in the belly of the whale.

As John thought more about his situation, tears began to roll down his face.

He said, "My Lord Jesus and my God, help me be strong. Give me the strength to survive their corruption." John cried himself to sleep.

As fate would have it, the following week, John was informed that he was selected by the Highway Patrol Capitol Police Division to be interviewed.

John was also informed that Mr. Henderlight was in the process of restoring the corporal rank back to him.

As fate would have it, John was hired by the highway patrol. He was assigned to the Capitol Police Division, and since he was already a state employee, it was a promotion for him.

John turned down the offer of being reinstated back to being a corporal. He believed it was Mr. Henderlight's way of trying to help him out before he left.

John turned in his resignation.

He wrote, "Mr. Henderlight, please accept my letter of resignation. You have given me an opportunity to be of service to these children again by rehiring me. You had promoted me. That's something I will never forget.

"Whether you may have realized it or not, a wrong was done to me in the past. You have corrected it. My heart will always be with the kids of SYC, and I want to say that it has been a pleasure to know you. I thank you for all that you have done for me. And good luck on your promotion."

As fate would have it, and to John's satisfaction, he smiled when he heard that the demons found out that he was going to be transferred to the highway patrol. They couldn't believe it.

BOOK ELEVEN

The State Capitol

In John's vision, he remembered the day when he transferred from Spencer Youth Center to the Highway Capitol Police Division. The year was 1989. He knew the Lord had intervened on his behalf.

As fate would have it, that was the year when his daughter was born.

Having that being said, at that time in John's vision, he still didn't know why he was transferred to the county in which he resided and why they feared him.

John was originally hired as a special agent until the title was changed to capitol police. It really didn't matter to him what the title of the position was. He was glad to have gotten away from SYC and those demons.

His duties were to protect and serve the state employees, state legislators, and the general public that visited the state offices as well as the capitol. His other duties were to make sure the state office buildings were locked and secured during and after business hours.

As a result of those duties, the other police officers from different agencies called the capitol police Door Shakers.

In response, John remembered saying on many occasions, "That's okay with me. One of these days, I'm going to shake open the door that will lead me to becoming a trooper."

Having that being said, with the exception of the patch, the capitol police uniform was the same as the state trooper uniform.

One patch said capitol police, and the other said state trooper, and from a distance, no one would have been able to tell the difference. That was what John liked about it the most.

As fate would have it, John was in the position to hear and see what actually took place behind those closed brass doors. He was able to see how the government operated from within and at the very top.

As time passed, John realized the same things that took place at the capitol where he was employed took place within the rest of the capitols. The only thing that was different was the name of the capitol.

He began to notice that the majority of everyone from the highest position to the lowest position acted as if they were better than one another because they worked at the capitol.

It reminded him of a cartoon that he had once seen. There was a hungry wolf that wanted to sneak down a hill toward a flock of sheep.

There has got to be a better way to getting close to those sheep without being recognized, the wolf said to himself.

The wolf thought of a plan. The wolf disguised himself as a sheep. He became a wolf in sheep clothing. The wolf's plan was working until it was discovered by the sheep that the wolf was indeed a wolf.

It just so happened as the wolf was crawling down the hill, a piece of the sheep's clothing that he wore got caught on a rock, and as the wolf got closer to the sheep, the sheep disguised came off.

As a result, the sheep were able to escape, and the wolf's true identity was known.

As fate would have it, John then realized that story reminded him of the position that he had found himself to be in. Somehow, he understood why the Lord in his wisdom had predestined him to work at the capitol. He was one of the Lord's sheep, and his position represented the wolf.

He believed the Lord purposely had him to be disguised outwardly as one of the wolves so that he wouldn't be recognized as being one of the Lord's sheep.

John's eyes were opened. He was able to see the good old boys for whom they really were. He was able to see how those of power and position manipulated each other and others. He was able to see the effects of favoritism, cronyism, corruption, injustice, retaliation, and racism.

John had noticed that the majority of the politicians that had sworn an oath didn't abide by the oath they had sworn to. They were more concerned with their own hidden agendas and advancing within the system than the promises they had made during their campaign.

John noticed that the government's system and mode of operation was all about favors, and the majority of those favors were conducted in secrete. And once one accepted the favor, that favor became the vise and/or the hook that one would use to control one another.

John noticed and he realized that was the trap one would find themselves once one accepted the favor. If one wouldn't continue to honor favors, the favor one had already accepted would be exposed, and as a result, one's future could be compromised. That was how their game was played.

John noticed and he realized that the majority of the laws created weren't really meant for the benefit of the citizens but for the benefit of themselves, meaning the good old boys.

John remembered seeing a bust of Nathan Forrest that was placed right before the door of the Legislative Chamber. He believed the majority of the legislators bowed down and paid homage to the bust as they entered the Legislative Chamber.

As fate would have it and as time passed, John began to feel like he was trapped. He was a witness. He knew the truth. He was able to see the good as well as the evil that lurked behind those closed doors. It reminded him of what he had read in his Bible. It was written that spiritual wickedness dwelled in high places, and as far as he was concerned, the capitol represented a high place.

In speaking of evil, John had always thought and had imagined that evil was something that was very frightening to look at. He realized how wrong he was. He had come to the realization that evil also hid behind pretty smiles, pretty faces, and those who wore half-opened blouses, short dresses, and nice suits and ties.

As fate would have it, John believed the evil ones had finally discovered that he wasn't one of them, and as a result, they came after him in full force. They wanted him terminated.

They began to write him up and accuse him of violating policies and procedures, and on several occasions, he was written up when he wasn't at work.

John would always challenge their write-ups through his chain of command, and he would always be exonerated. It had gotten to the point that the assistant commissioner of the highway patrol had notified the director at the capitol and had instructed him not to write John up unless he had permission from his office to do so.

John believed that was the straw that broke the camel's back. He knew then that they really hated him.

As fate would have it, as a result of John's vision, he was able to see and understand why the evil ones hated him. He understood why the Lord had placed him in the midst of "the system of things."

He believed the Lord had placed him within the system of government so that his will would be done. John knew the tactics, policies, procedures, rules, regulations, and the laws.

Having that being said, it brought back memories to he when he was in college. He thought about the events that had taken place during the civil rights movement that involved Rev. Martin Luther King Jr., Malcolm X, and others that had taken a stand for justice. They fought from the outside of the system.

John then realized that it was meant for him to fight from the inside of the system.

John remembered something that he had read in the King James Version of the Bible. The Lord said Peter would deny him three times before the rooster would crow.

As fate would have it, he believed the Lord had taken him back to that day and time. He suddenly understood why. He believed he saw the fear in Peter's eyes.

Peter was in fear of his own life. Peter was a true witness. He had seen what the system of government in that day and time had done to Jesus. He knew by acknowledging that he was a follower of Jesus, he would have suffered the same and/or similar fate that was to come to Jesus. Peter was afraid of what man would do to him.

As fate would have it, John had come to the realization that the system in the Lord's day and time, along with its demons, with all its might, power, and ability to carry out the crucifixion of Jesus, that system and its demons, couldn't break the faith that Jesus had in his father.

And as a result, that system and its demons had become fearful of not only the Lord personally but of his faith.

John believed the faith that Jesus had was more powerful than Peter's fear of man. John believed the faith that he had in Jesus, and the faith Jesus had in his *father*, was what the system and the evil ones feared the most.

As fate would have it, John had come to the realization that fear was the greatest weapon of mass destruction, and having faith in the Lord was the greatest weapon against fear.

John had also come to the realization that the fear that was within the world was like a rim on the wheel of a bicycle. It revolved around and around and around continuously.

John believed each spoke on the rim represented the ills of the world. He believed racism was the most evil spoke of them all. He believed history had revealed and had established that fact, specifically within America.

John believed America, with all its greatness, unfortunately was built upon racism, and the zeal to be number one had caused a devastating domino effect, which he believed had caused a father to turn against one's own father, a mother turn against one's own mother, a brother turn against one's own brother, a sister turn against one's own sister, a friend turn against one's own friend, a relative turn against one's own relative, and an enemy turn to one's own enemy.

As fate would have it, John finally understood why those evil ones were afraid of him. They feared the faith that he had in the Lord more than the dislike of the color of his skin.

John finally understood why he was transferred to the county in which he resided. He realized that the evil ones couldn't fire him, and they felt that he wouldn't quit. So they set in motion a plan to terminate him and/or to get him to quit in another way.

Book Twelve

Their Plan

I n John's vision, he remembered when he was promoted and was sent to the county in which he resided. He didn't know at the time that he was the only Black trooper in the entire district.

Having that being said, as a result of being promoted to the trooper position, he was placed on probation again. He knew it would be easier for the department to terminate him.

As John thought about that in his vision, he didn't know exactly how they were going to try to terminate him.

One of the primary functions of a trooper was to write tickets. The troopers were evaluated by their performance and productivity in doing so.

It just so happened the evil ones had John to ride with each trooper of his post for a total of three months. They never gave him a ticket book.

Having that being said, after three months had passed, John was finally set free to patrol by himself.

That was a day that he could hardly wait to come. He enjoyed being on his own. He was able to make his own decisions, and whenever he was in town, he would look at the reflection of himself and his patrol car off the windows of the businesses as he drove by. That made him smile.

As fate would have it, John and his girlfriend had gotten married. It was three months after he had arrived in the county. He had been waiting for that day to come. That also made him smile.

During the first two weeks that John was on his own, his sergeant approached him. John could tell by the expression on his face that he seemed to be very concerned.

John remembered his sergeant saying to him, "John, wouldn't you be more comfortable being in another district where there are other Black troopers?"

John had already discovered that he was the only Black trooper in the district. He actually enjoyed that fact. He knew that every eye was going to be focused on him, and he realized that whatever he would do and/or say would become history because of that fact.

John thought about what his sergeant had said. John then said to himself, *I'm not going to let you run me out of town. If and when I may decide to leave, it will be because I want to leave.*

As fate would have it, John's sergeant also said to him, "John, you are going to have to go to the main headquarters with the captain."

The main headquarters was in Davidson County, and that was where the capitol was.

John had been working long enough to know that the only time a trooper went to the main headquarters with their captain was when one was being promoted and/or fired.

He knew he hadn't done anything to be promoted and/or to be fired.

So he said to his sergeant, "Why do I have to go to headquarters?"

The sergeant responded by saying, "I don't know why. You might want to ask the lieutenant."

He then asked his lieutenant the same question, and the lieutenant said, "I don't know why. Ask your sergeant."

John knew then that he was in trouble. The only thing he didn't know was why he had to go.

As fate would have it, two weeks had gone by, and on a Friday morning, John's captain came to drive him to headquarters. He had a smile on his face as if he had won the lottery.

John wasn't smiling. He was upset. He said in a loud tone of voice, "Captain, I was born and raised within the Military. I was raised to treat everyone equally regardless of one's skin color."

John's captain smiled and responded by saying, "I was raised the same way."

John then said in a loud, demanding tone of voice, "Then why do I have to go to headquarters?"

John had caught his captain off guard. His captain hesitated, and then he cleared his throat and said, "Well, John, we feel like you haven't been productive."

After hearing that, a smile came upon John's face. He said quietly to himself, *You had just put a nail in your own coffin. I am going to bury you.*

As fate would have it, John and his captain finally arrived, and after they entered the building, they went to a meeting room. And to John's surprise, he noticed that the commissioner and all his commanders were there. He also saw other troopers in that room with their captains. The other troopers looked as if they were about to be hanged.

It just so happened John and his captain were the last ones to get there. Everyone was waiting on them.

After John and his captain sat down, the commissioner stood up and said to all the troopers that were there with their captains, including John, "Your captains have brought you all here because they feel like you haven't been productive. There are three things that I can do to you. I can demote you, transfer you out of the department, and/or I can fire you. If there is anything that you need to say, now is the time to say it."

John looked around the room, and he noticed that his captain was smiling, and the other troopers looked as if they had given up their ghost. They didn't say a word.

As fate would have it, John raised his hand, and that was when the commissioner said, "Trooper, what is on your mind?"

That was what John was waiting on and was hoping the commissioner would say. John stood up, and he looked straight at the commissioner. One could hear a pin drop. Every eye was looking at John. John also noticed that his captain wasn't smiling anymore. John almost burst out laughing when he had seen the expression on his captain's face.

John purposely pointed his finger at his captain, and as a result, everyone in the room turned around and looked at his captain.

John then said, "Commissioner, they didn't give me an opportunity to produce activity. They made me ride with the other troopers for a total of three months. They never gave me a ticket book."

One could hear a pin drop again. He looked at his captain again. He could have sworn he saw horns protrude from his captain's head. His face and neck appeared to be red as fire. It took all that John had within him to not burst out laughing.

The commissioner and all his commanders turned around, and they stared at John's captain again. The commissioner also turned red, and he had a look upon his face as if he wanted to fire John's captain on the spot.

The commissioner then looked at John and said, "John, you can look at this as constructive criticism."

John realized, and he noticed that the commissioner said John instead of trooper. John knew then that he had gained respect from his commissioner, and that made him smile.

John responded by saying, "Yes, sir."

Having that being said, the commissioner then looked at John's captain and said, "Captain, meet me in my office."

As fate would have it, the ride back to John's county was very quiet. His captain tried his best to be nice to him. He offered to buy John something to eat, and his attitude was awful kind.

John responded by saying, "No, thank you."

Actually, John wanted to say something else that wouldn't have been Christian like.

As fate would have it, John then realized that his captain's plan had failed. In fact, his captain's plan turned out to be a blessing.

John knew they couldn't bring him again to headquarters unless he had really done something wrong, and even if they did, he had plan to say he was being retaliated against which would have been true.

John finally realized how they were going to try to fire him. He also knew that they weren't finished. He knew he had to be somewhat perfect.

As time passed, John had gained a reputation as being one that would arrest his own mother among other things. John actually enjoyed his reputation. He was well-known as being an honest cop, and he treated everyone equal. People trusted him as well as being afraid to get pulled over by him. The majority knew if he had pulled them over, they were guilty of committing a traffic violation and/or the law.

What the majority didn't know was the fact that just because he would pull them over, it didn't mean that they were going to receive a ticket and/or was going to be placed under arrest.

Having that being said, John's reputation had gotten to the point where the criminals respected him. They knew if they did something wrong in front of him, he would do his job, and once that was done, he wouldn't use what they had done against them by harassing them later.

John had actually helped a lot of people without being asked to. That way, he didn't owe anyone any favors, and they didn't owe him any. He was strict as well as compassionate toward people whether they knew it or not.

As time passed, people began to call and would write letters to John's superiors. They would express their appreciation of him being straight and not showing favoritism. Several people had called him and said, "John, I work for so and so. I sell drugs. If anything ever happens to me, I wanted someone to know and that's you."

At times, John wondered why they called him. He hadn't asked for that information.

Having that being said, John knew those people that had called him worked for people who were in power, and those people had political connections. He also believed those people knew that he knew who they were.

As time passed, John remembered in his vision he had a vision, and in his vision, he *imagined* hearing an angel say to him, *The Lord wants you to run for governor.*

John thought about that. He said to himself, *Governor! I don't have any money to run for governor. I don't know anyone!*

John hadn't expressed a desire to run for any political office because of the things that he had seen and heard when he worked at the capitol.

Having that being said, John had learned from past experience to do what he believed the Lord wanted him to do.

As a result, he submitted a memo through his chain of command requesting permission to run for governor.

John imagined what his superiors was going to say once they received his memo. He *imagined* seeing them laughing and saying, *What! Now, he wants to be our boss!*

John received a response from his superiors in three days. It read, "Trooper Robinson, the Office of Governor is a partisan position. You would have to resign your position as a trooper to pursue that endeavor."

John thought about that, and he said to himself, *I can't quit my job. I'm going to run for county commissioner. That position isn't a partisan position.*

John then submitted his memo through his chain of command, and he requested permission to run for county commissioner. He received a response in less than two weeks. He was given permission to do so.

Having that being said, it just so happened John lived in the Fifth District, which was considered to be a well-to-do White middle-class neighborhood.

Having that being said, the county in which John lived had about eight other areas within it called districts, and there were two commissioners per district.

It just so happened there was a deputy sheriff who was one of the two commissioners in his district.

As fate would have it, on Election Day, the votes were not all counted. The votes weren't counted and/or completed in two districts.

It just so happened John's district was one of them, and the other district was where another deputy sheriff lived and who was also a commissioner. The current county sheriff lived in that district as well.

It was said that John lost by eleven votes and that a county deputy had taken the results to the Election Office, which would have been illegal.

John didn't contest or challenge the results. He considered it to be his first lesson as being a casualty of dirty politics.

As time passed, in his vision, he remembered July 2007. That was when the sheriff and Terry had already begun to campaign for sheriff, which was to be in 2010. John decided that he wanted to run for sheriff.

The sheriff position wasn't a partisan position, and being that the sheriff and Terry had already gotten an early start, John wanted to get an early start too. He submitted a memo through his chain of command expressing his desire to run for sheriff.

As fate would have it, three months after John had submitted his memo, he hadn't received a response. He knew then that something was going on behind the scenes. He knew if he started his campaign without being given permission to, his department could use that as a way to fire him.

John believed the reason they hadn't responded went beyond the color of his skin and/or his faith.

By being the sheriff, John would have access to the archives. He had already written two books, and he had named the real names in his second book.

John *imagined* the possibility of them saying, *If he becomes the sheriff, he will start digging through the archives, and he would write another book about what he would discover.*

John then remembered what he was told and what he had read about the race riot that had taken place in the county and what was said about the highway patrol's involvement.

It was said that the highway patrol had committed many unjustifiable acts against the Black citizens during that time.

John *imagined* them also saying, *We can't take a chance on him being elected. If we do something to him physically, people will believe we had something to do with it because of the books he wrote. We got to be clever about this.*

John believed they were hoping he would begin campaigning without being given permission to do so. John decided to submit another memo through his chain of command requesting permission to run for sheriff.

He said, "Maybe you lost the first one, so here is another one."

In the meantime, a county commissioner had passed away in John's district. It wasn't the deputy. His name was Jackson.

It just so happened it was the custom to allow the spouse of the deceased to continue in the position until the next election. In doing so was another example of the good old boy way of doing things, which wasn't legal either.

It just so happened the deceased spouse was too ill to undertake the position. It was the first time that situation had happened.

John tried to contact Jackson by phone. Jackson didn't respond, so John left a message on Jackson's phone saying, "Jackson, you know that I am the one that campaign for that position and that I am the one that should finish out the term, especially being that I only lost by eleven votes."

As fate would have it, a week had passed, and John still didn't get a response from Jackson.

Having that being said, it just so happened one day, John was reading the newspaper when he saw an ad soliciting a response from anyone that would be interested in the vacant commissioner's position in the Fifth District and for that person to fill out and send in a résumé.

As time passed and while in secrete, the evil ones had selected another county employee to fill that vacant position, and they had set a date for that person to be sworn in.

The person they selected was the director of the grand jury. John knew the person, and he found out the date and time.

John showed up during the conformation ceremony. He noticed on the program that the conformation was to be the first order of business. That changed when they noticed that John was there. They waited to the very end.

The mayor stood up, and he announced the name of the person they were about to swear in. He also had to say, "Is there anyone present that objects?"

John raised his hand, and when he stood up, one could hear a pin drop. He walked up to the podium. He took his time, and he looked into everyone's eyes, especially the few Black commissioners that were present.

John then said, "Every one of you had sworn an oath. You all know you are wrong. You should be ashamed of yourself. I really have nothing against the person you have chosen.

"You all know that I am the one that should have been chosen. I am the one who legally ran for office."

As fate would have it, several commissioners blame it on the deputy/commissioner, Jackson. They said he was the one that had made the recommendation.

John said quietly to himself, *They don't want me in any position that would give me an opportunity to know what they do behind closed doors.*

As John thought about that, he smiled as he *imagined* seeing himself walking among them and them looking as if they had seen a ghost.

As fate would have it, seven more months had passed, and John still hadn't received a response giving him permission to run for sheriff. It was March 2008. So he decided to send an email.

It just so happened two days after John had sent his email, he was told to report to his district headquarters. John reported to his district headquarters along with his newly promoted lieutenant. His name was Bray. John's captain had just got off the phone, talking to his superiors at the main headquarters.

He said, "John, I just got off the phone talking to headquarters. I was told to tell you why you were told to report here. We called you here so that there won't be a misunderstanding. We received your memos and your email. If you run for sheriff, we are going to transfer you based upon a policy that says, 'Any trooper that runs for any elected office has to temporarily transfer out of the county where the election takes place.'"

John was put in a hell of a spot. Troopers have been running for sheriff as long as he could remember, and they were not transferred out of the county based upon a policy of which he was just told.

John knew his captain was expecting him to give him an answer on whether or not he was going to run for sheriff. The problem he had about answering was the fact that he knew there was no such policy, and he knew his captain knew he knew it didn't exist.

He knew if he said he was going to run for sheriff, they were going to transfer him out of the county based upon a policy that didn't exist, and if he said that he wasn't going to run, then it would have been all over with. He believed that was what they were expecting him to say.

John felt himself being under a tremendous amount of pressure. He didn't know what to do and/or say. He prayed quietly, and he said, "Lord, I don't know what to do and/or say."

As fate would have it, John *imagined* the Lord saying to him, *Don't say anything.*

John knew his captain had to report back to his superiors to tell them his response. John didn't say anything, and that was when he left the office.

As time passed, on January 5, 2009, John had made his official announcement to run for sheriff.

As fate would have it, three hours later, John received orders saying that he was being transferred out of the county.

As a result, he had become the first trooper in the history of the highway patrol to be transferred out of the county as a result of running for an elected office that was based upon a policy that didn't exist.

Book Thirteen

I Took a Stand

As a result of John's vision, he finally understood why he was transferred, and after he thought about it, he *imagined* how upset they must to have been at him.

The department couldn't force him to quit in spite of everything they had done to him.

John believed as a result of him wanting to get involved in the election process as a candidate, that really scared them.

He believed they knew he had a chance of winning the sheriff race, and it would have been too obvious for them to force him to physically move out of his county. So they decided to change his duty assignment.

As fate would have it, that was what John was thinking about and what had kept him from going to sleep after the sheriff race was over.

He believed the department's original intention was to transfer him as far away from the county in which he resided to a county where it would have taken him a long time to travel back and forth to work and his home.

As fate would have it, a trooper who lived in the county next to John had requested an emergency transfer. His father had gotten sick, and that trooper's father lived in another district.

It just so happened the trooper was able to make an emergency transfer to that district where his father lived, and as a result, it left an opening in that county where he had left.

John's department had no choice but to send him to that county. The county was Marshall County.

Having that being said, and knowing that John only lived about ten minutes from the Marshall County line, John believed the department added an additional order to the transfer order that he had received.

It read, "You cannot come back to your home county until your shift was over."

That meant he couldn't cross over the county line to come home to eat and/or to be with his family until his shift was over, and as a result, he not only had become the first trooper to be transferred out of the county as a result of running for an elected office. He became the first trooper that couldn't come home until his shift was over.

John believed the department would go as far as to have someone to hide at all the entrances that would lead him back into his home county in attempt to see if he would cross over the county line before his shift was over.

Having that being said, John remembered the first day he had crossed over the county line to go to work. He didn't know the territory. It was like he had to start over.

John was upset about that. He thought and said quietly, *I am going to do just enough to get by. I hope someday the department is going to need me to go to my home county to work a wreck or something. I am not going to obey that order no matter what happens. That includes if someone robs a bank or worst.*

As time passed, John felt alone. He didn't know the troopers in Marshall County personally. He knew he couldn't tell them anything about his situation without it being repeated.

As fate would have it, John met a city police officer. The officer's name was McClain. McClain was Hispanic. He had faced similar racial experiences that John had faced.

John believed the Lord had a hand in him meeting McClain. McClain was someone whom John felt confrontable with. John liked and trusted him.

John remembered one early morning he was in his patrol car. He was alone in an empty parking lot of a shopping center. He was in town when McClain drove up beside him. McClain was in his patrol car.

McClain looked at John and said, "Hey, son, where have you been? What's wrong?"

He could tell John had a lot on his mind. John was thinking about what his department had recently done to him. John didn't know what he was going to do about it. He was thinking of a strategy.

McClain already knew the reason why John was transferred. John had already told him about that.

"Man, the reason you hadn't seen me in a while is because the department had suspended me for ten days. They said I had violated policy by campaigning while on duty.

"They said I had violated the Little Hatch Act. They also had the nerve to say if I appealed their decision and won, I could get my time and pay back.

"The department knew it was going to be hard for me to effectively campaign for sheriff while being out of the county. The sheriff and a local fireman in my county had the opportunity to be seen and heard while they were on duty and while they both were in uniform. They have the advantage!

"The department knew by me being out of the county, I would be out of sight and out of mind. I believed that was part of their plan so it would be easier for the sheriff to be reelected.

"The department accused me of campaigning on duty because I had ordered and had brought campaign material while on duty here."

It just so happened John was reading copies of his general orders that pertained to political activity when McClain arrived. He handed them to McClain to look at.

One copy read, "The Little Hatch Act prohibits public officers and employees from (1) using their official position, authority, or influence to interfere with an election or nomination for office or directly or indirectly attempt to intimidate, coerce, or command any other officer or employee to vote for or against any measure, party, or person or knowingly receive or pay assessments of any kind or character for political purpose or for election expenses from any other officer or employee; (2) directly or indirectly depriving, attempting to deprive, or threatening to deprive any person of employment, position, work, compensation, contracts, loans, grants, appropriations, or benefits provided from public funds for any political activity in support of or opposition to any candidate, party, or measure in any elections; and (3) displaying political material in state-owned controlled buildings or on state-owned land or vehicles."

"John, they transferred you out of the county, and there isn't anything in your general orders that states you had to be transferred out of your county as a result of running for an elected office.

"The campaign material you ordered and brought wasn't displayed in or outside of your patrol car. They didn't give you an opportunity to contest the charge of violating your general orders when they suspended you.

"The general order that pertains to transfers says, 'Transfers may be used as disciplinary action if it is determined by the appointing authority that an employee's ability to satisfactorily perform his/her duties is beyond the capabilities of the employee or the employee has been compromised by notorious conduct to the extent that he/she is ineffective in his/her position.

"'In these instances, the employee may be demoted or transferred to a position that is more appropriate after minimum due process has been provided.'

"In these cases, your department was the ones that violated your general orders. You didn't do anything wrong. I believe you got them," McClain said.

As fate would have it, a smile came upon John's face. He said, "McClain, you're right."

John believed the Lord knew what he needed. It was for someone else to know and say to him what he knew all along. McClain was that person. John set in motion *to take a stand.*

Having that being said, after John's shift was over and as soon as he got home, he sat down and wrote everything he could remember that involved him during and after the election. He planned a strategy and what he was going to do and say in his defense.

John wrote and said in his *opening statement*, "I was born and raised within a military environment.

"At the age of eighteen, I wasn't drafted. I joined the Army during the Vietnam War. I was a military policeman.

"I had also served as a combat military policeman in the Army National Guard.

"I was a deputy sheriff for one year while pursuing a bachelor of science degree in criminal justice, and I had since obtained that degree as well as an associate degree in digital audio production.

"I have written two novels that were published, and I had just recently received a plaque from the past governor acknowledging my thirty years of loyal and dedicated service to this state.

"I had served this state as a supervisor in a state juvenile correctional institution, and at this present time, I have been protecting and serving the citizens of this state as a state trooper for the past twenty-three years.

"The point I am trying to make is that I have served honorably in my profession, all of my career, and now I have found myself in the position to where I am forced to defend the integrity of my good name and reputation.

"The department had accused me of violating general orders and policies that pertained to political activity and had suspended me for ten days without pay.

"The department said that my conduct was unbecoming and that I showed deception, illustrated a disregard for departmental policies and procedures, and had put the department in a bad light by my actions.

"I will show that the department, by their own hands, showed deception, had illustrated a disregard for departmental policies and procedures, and had put themselves in a bad light by their own actions.

"I will show that the department had tainted this case and had committed an offense far worse than what they have accused me of.

"I intend to prove that as a result of my filing a discrimination and retaliation charge against the department, the department had waged a personal vendetta against me.

"I will show that the department with its power of influence had conspired, plotted, and violated my constitutional rights and had interfered and lessened my chances of being successful in the 2010 sheriff's race by transferring me out of the county.

"I will show the department's actions in this case from the very beginning was designed to defame my character, to punish me, and to set me up to be terminated.

"I will show that I was denied the full benefit of due process of the law prior to, during, and after I had appeared before the department's due process hearings.

"Furthermore, I will show that the EEOC and the Civil Service Commission was bias and had shown favoritism for the benefit of the department. They had failed to take in consideration the totality of the whole case, the facts, and reasoning. They sided with the department."

John also added a *chronological order of events* that had taken place to wit:

"(1) On October 23, 2005, I had followed policy and procedure. I sent a notice to my superiors announcing my intentions to be a candidate in the 2006 gubernatorial race, and in October 26, I received a response from my superiors stating that I could not be a candidate in a partisan race while being employed by the department. I didn't pursue that endeavor.

"(2) In February 2006, I sent a notice to my superiors announcing my intentions to be a candidate in the county commissioner race, and on April 3, 2006, I received a certified letter from my colonel advising me that I wasn't violating the Little Hatch Act and that it was okay for me to be a candidate in county commissioner race.

"(3) On July 22, 2007, I submitted a letter to my superiors announcing my intention to be a candidate in the 2010 sheriff's race. I didn't receive a response in a timely manner.

"(4) On January 2, 2008, I had submitted another memo to my superiors expressing my intention to be a candidate in the 2010 sheriff's race. I didn't get a response then either.

"In the meantime, I had gotten holed of a letter that someone had sent to the Attorney General seeking the advice whether or not a state trooper could run for sheriff without violating the Federal Hatch Act.

"Having that being said, the opinion was given on September 10, 2008. The analysis stated in quote, 'A state trooper has expressed an interest in running for the office of sheriff. You have asked whether this would be in violation of the Federal Hatch Act.

"'Whether the Federal Hatch Act applies to the state trooper in question would, thus, depend on whether the trooper's position is in connection with an activity financed in whole or in part by federal loans or grants.'

"Having that being said, that was an indication to me that something was set in motion to stop me from running for sheriff and/or winning.

"(5) On March 19, 2008, I sent an email to my superiors announcing my intention to be a candidate to run for sheriff, and that was when I was told to report to my district headquarters.

"After I arrived at my district headquarters, my captain said, 'John, I was told per my superiors to tell you that we received your memos and your email, and the reason why you were told to be here today was so that there would be no misunderstanding.'

"That alone was admission and proof that the department had violated general orders by not replying to my requests in a timely manner.

"My captain said, 'If you were to pursue being a candidate in the 2010 sheriff's race, you will be temporarily transferred out of your county based upon policy that says, "It is the policy of the department that any trooper that runs for an elected office, the trooper has to be temporarily transferred out of the county in which the election takes place, and that policy has been implemented throughout the state."'"

"In my opinion, that was a threat. Troopers have been running for sheriff ever since I was employed by the department, and to my knowledge, no trooper has ever been told that they had to be transferred out of their county as a result of running for an elected office.

"Having that being said, every trooper in the state has to sign every general order to verify one's knowledge of receiving that order. I had never seen and/or had signed such policy and/or order.

"(6) On May 16, 2008, I had exercised my constitutional rights by filing a racial discrimination and retaliation complaint with the EEOC against my department.

"And prior to doing that, I went to a local newspaper company in my county, and I told a reporter that my department was going to transfer me out of the county as a result of me running for sheriff.

"(7) On June 29, 2008, an article was written in the local newspaper that pertained to my statement.

"The highway patrol's director of communication had responded and said, 'The department requires any employee campaigning for any office to transfer out of the county where the election is taking place. It is implemented statewide. Our policy is if you are running for office, you can't work in the same county where you're running for office.'

"As fate would have it, the director's response had been publicized, and as a result, their untruth had been written for all to see.

"(8) On November 6, 2008, I received a response that was in the form of a letter from the EEOC. It said, 'Evidence obtained during the investigation revealed that no one has requested to run for an elected office since May 2006, except Trooper Robinson.

"'Evidence fails to show that others have been transferred out of the county in which they were running for office.

"'Evidence shows Trooper Robinson had run for an office and was not required to transfer to another county. There are no other similarly situated employees.

"'The respondent contents that it has been the practice of the department to temporarily reassign duties to an adjoining county, and that practice has not been written into any of the department's general orders or policy.'

"Having that being said, that was my point. But yet nothing was done to the department by the EEOC as a result of me being transferred out of the county.

"(9) On December 22, 2008, my superiors finally gave me permission to announce my candidacy and said upon my announcement for candidacy, I would be temporarily transferred to another county.

"(10) On January 5, 2010, just three hours after I had made my announcement to run for sheriff, I was transferred out of the county.

"I believed as a result of the nonaction of the EEOC, the department took that as a sign that it was okay for them to transfer me out of the county."

Having that being said, there were five appeal processes that John was afforded by his department and by law. He couldn't afford to retain an attorney at that time. He needed his available funds to help pay for his daughter's tuition as she prepared to go to a law school in Florida. John represented himself.

The department conducted John's first appeal. He had to appear before a captain and a few other ranking members of his department.

In John's opinion, having to retain legal counsel wouldn't have done him any good, and it would have been a waste of money.

The captain began the hearing by saying, "Trooper Robinson, you are here because you had violated general orders and policy by campaigning while on duty."

John responded by saying, "No. I am here because you transferred me out of the county as a result of me running for an elected office."

Needless to say, that remark didn't set well with them. They didn't want to talk about that. John lost his first appeal.

As time passed, John appeared before another captain of his department. That was to be his second appeal.

The captain said, "Trooper Robinson, you are here as a result of you violating general orders and policy. You were given an opportunity to have a fair hearing during your first appeal, and you had lost."

John's second appeal lasted less than ten minutes. He wasn't allowed to give his side of the story. John lost that appeal as well.

As time passed, John appeared before an administrative law judge of the Civil Service Commission. That was to be his third appeal.

Before the hearing began, John noticed that the judge was staring at the gold badges that his superiors were wearing on their uniform. She then looked at John and said, "How come you don't have a gold badge?"

John knew then that she was bought and paid for.

She began the hearing by saying, "My name is Judge Mary. I am here on behalf of the highway patrol."

Having that being said and after she had thought about what she had said, she corrected herself by saying, "I mean the Civil Service Commission."

The slip of the tongue was no excuse. The judge had verified John's suspicion.

John said to his captain, who was placed under oath, "Tell me about the general order and policy pertaining to political activity."

John's captain responded by saying, "It is the policy of the department that says any trooper that runs for an elected office has to temporarily transfer out of the county, and that policy has been implemented throughout the state."

John smiled after hearing what his captain had just said. John then stared at his captain. John hesitated before he said to his captain, "Show me a copy of that general order."

John's captain then said, "We don't have a policy. It is an unwritten policy."

Having that being said, John's captain committed perjury while under oath, and John still lost.

As time passed, John appeared before the full Civil Service Commission Board. That was to be his fourth appeal. The hearing only lasted about twenty minutes. They took sides with the department.

John lost all his state appeals. He only had one more shot left, which was to be heard in the Chancery Court. John hired an attorney.

As time passed, John appeared in the Chancery Court. It was his last opportunity and chance. John remembered when he entered the courtroom, he noticed that the department's attorney was already talking to the judge. It appeared to him that they were friends. The judge gave everyone verbal instructions on how she planned to proceed.

The department's lawyer spoke first. She said, "The reason we are here today is because the department had suspended Trooper Robinson for ten days as a result of him violating general orders and policy by campaigning while on duty."

John's attorney spoke up and said, "As a result of the Progressive Punishment Law, the ten-day suspension given to my client was in excess of the normal amount of punishment given due to the nature of the charge of which my client was accused of."

The judge responded by saying, "I am very aware of the law. Do you mean to tell me if someone breaks the law, I am to pat that person on the hand and let him go?"

John believed after hearing that, she apparently didn't know anything about his case.

John's attorney then said, "None of this would have taken place if my client wasn't transferred illegally."

As fate would have it, the judge then said, "What do you mean by that?"

John's attorney explained what had happened, and that was when the judge said, "Hmm, that sounds very interesting. I will have to take this case under advisement. I will get back with you in two weeks."

Having that being said, John felt his heart beating again. He said, "Now I know she didn't know anything about my case."

John couldn't wait for the two weeks to pass, and it did, and he still hadn't heard anything from the court. John believed the judge was finally looking into his case.

Having that being said, two months had passed, and John still hadn't heard anything about the status of his case. And as a result, he began to worry.

As fate would have it, a new governor of the state was elected. He was a wealthy businessman.

The first thing he had done was to abolish the Civil Service Commission. He said the commission wasn't effective.

John believed the governor's real reason for doing so was so that he could have more power. The governor did other things for personal gains as well. He was no better than the majority of the others.

As far as abolishing the Civil Service Commission, it was a good thing for John and a bad thing for the rest of the government employees.

Having that being said, a total of three months had gone by, and John still hadn't heard anything from his attorney about his case, and he knew there was nothing that he could do about it.

As fate would have it, one Sunday morning while John was at church, there was a guest speaker there.

John's pastor said, "John, will you take care of the needs of the guest speaker?"

John had never done anything like that before. He hadn't had time to be involved in church activities because of his work schedule. He was told that he could sit in the area where the preacher preached. That also was his first time.

As time passed and after the preacher finished his sermon, he went straight to John's daughter and said, "The Lord told me to tell you to not worry about friends. He will take care of you."

That prophecy got John's attention. He didn't believe in coincidences. His daughter was about to go to Barry School of Law in Florida. John thought his daughter might have been wondering about that.

John then observed the preacher walking back and forth and saying, "Someone in here is going through some thing."

After hearing that, John said quietly to himself, *What kind of prophecy is that? Everybody is going through something.*

John then noticed the preacher walking toward him and saying, "I don't know who it is, but it is big."

The preacher stood and had leaned on the podium. He looked as if he was in deep thought as he looked toward the congregation.

He had his right hand under his chin, and he was shaking his head. Then all of a sudden, he turned, and he looked at John. He stared at John.

John didn't know what to do. The expression on the preacher's face had concerned him.

Then the preacher pointed his finger at John and said, "It's you! I don't know why. The Lord told me to point my finger at you and to tell you to keep on having faith in him."

After hearing that prophecy, John really didn't know what to say. So he said, "I will."

As fate would have it, the following morning at 8:00, John had received a phone call from his attorney. His attorney said, "John, you won your case. You will be receiving the results shortly in the mail."

Having that being said, John smiled, and he thanked the Lord. John said, "Finally! After all these years, I have won."

As time passed, John received the results and the decision of the court. It was the conformation and proof that he was waiting on. He needed it so that he could prepare to file a lawsuit against his department.

BOOK FOURTEEN

The Documents of the Court

John could hardly wait to receive the court's decision. He checked his mailbox every day. To him, it was like waiting for a check to arrive.

As fate would have it, the day came. John retrieved a package from his mailbox. He was excited. He smiled as he opened the package. It contained the Chancery Court documents and orders.

One document was titled "The Memorandum and Order." It said in quote, "The petitioner, Mr. John Robinson, seeks judicial review of a decision by the Civil Service Commission. The commission upheld the highway patrol's decision to suspend Mr. Robinson for ten days without pay for engaging in political activity.

"Mr. Robinson submits that the decision to discipline him violated statutory provisions, was made in an improper manner and upon unlawful procedures, was unsupported by substantial and material evidence, and was a clearly unwarranted exercise of discretion.

"The court has reviewed the technical record, the pleadings, the exhibits, and the briefs filed on behalf of the parties.

"For the following reasons, the court reverses the decision of the commission and Mr. Robinson's ten-day suspension without pay."

The "Factual and Procedural Background Document" stated in quote, "Mr. Robinson has served as a highway patrol officer for over twenty-three years. In 2006, he qualified to run for county commissioner in a nonpartisan election.

"On April 3, 2006, Highway Patrol Colonel Walker sent him a letter stating that his candidacy was permissible with the following caveats: He could not hold himself out as a member of a particular party, he could not accept funds from a particular party, he could not be endorsed by a particular party, and he could not participate in any activity that may be deemed partisan.

"On May 15, 2006, the department declared in a general order that its policy was to 'allow and accommodate transfer requests by employees when such request is determined to be beneficial to the department and the employees.'

"On December 22, 2008, Captain Steven wrote to Mr. Robinson that he had permission to announce his candidacy for the 2010 sheriff's race and would be temporarily assigned to another county for the good of the department and to avoid any political conflicts within his home county.

"On January 6, 2009, Mr. Robinson qualified to run for sheriff in a nonpartisan election. During his campaign, Mr. Robinson purchased campaign signs from the Wintzel Sign Shop. Mr. Robinson acknowledged that he went to the sign shop in his patrol car while wearing his uniform and picked up at least two of his signs, placed them in his patrol car, drove to meet his wife, and placed the signs in her car.

"The affidavit of the shop owner, Mrs. Wintzel, stated that Mr. Robinson came to the shop in uniform on several occasions while on duty to order banners and later pay and pick up his magnetic campaign signs.

"In or around late October 2009, the owner of the sign shop contacted Mr. Robinson's supervisor, Sergeant Logan, complaining that Mr. Robinson had not completed payment for the signs and asking if Mr. Robinson's wages could be garnished to pay the outstanding amount.

"As a result of this phone call, the department assigned a sergeant officer of the Professional Responsibility Division to investigate the complaint.

"On Sunday, November 1, 2009, while on duty, Mr. Robinson called the sign shop to see if he could pick up his signs that day. He spoke to Mrs. Wintzel's children who said that Mrs. Wintzel was not at home but that she had relayed a message that he could come by her shop the following morning and pick up his signs.

"Mrs. Wintzel called Mr. Robinson's supervisor and reported the conversation.

"On Monday, November 2, 2009, the sergeant officer photographed Mr. Robinson when he arrived at the sign shop while on duty in his uniform and in his patrol car. The sergeant officer observed Mr. Robinson first enter the sign shop and then exit with two campaign banners, place them in his patrol car, and finally drive off with the campaign banners in his car.

"After a review of the sergeant officer's report, Captain Steven determined that Mr. Robinson had committed violations of departmental policies and procedures and recommended that Mr. Robinson be given a substantial suspension.

"On January 1, 2010, using the highway patrol's discipline matrix, Lieutenant Colonel Tracy recommended that Colonel Walker suspend Mr. Robinson for ten days without pay for five different occasions of political activity that violated the statute and the department's policies. On January 20, 2010, Colonel Walker concurred in the recommended discipline.

"Mr. Robinson appealed the disciplinary decision. He requested a due process level III hearing that Director Hogan conducted on February 2, 2010.

"At the hearing, Mr. Robinson denied that he had approached an individual, Johnston, for support two years earlier and asked why the 2007 claim was presented in 2009.

"Mr. Robinson asserted that he was being denied a fair due process hearing and that he was accused of actions that were going to destroy his reputation. He denied conduct unbecoming an officer, repeating that the only thing he did was to purchase the campaign signs and put them in his vehicle for ten minutes until he could give them to his wife because he knew that he should not have them in his patrol car.

"Director Hogan took the matter under advisement and issued a memorandum on February 11, 2010, concurring with the recommended discipline of a ten-day suspension without pay.

"The record does not reflect that Mr. Robinson ever received a copy of the complaint prior to the hearing or that Mr. Robinson was afforded a timely opportunity to confront the individual who claimed that Mr. Robinson solicited his support in 2007.

"On March 8, 2010, Mr. Robinson requested a level IV grievance hearing, and on March 17, 2010, Captain Brown, the designated hearing manager, conducted the level IV hearing and concurred with the recommendation of Colonel Walker.

"Mr. Robinson requested a level V hearing before the commission, which was held on November 4, 2010. On May 16, 2011, administrative law judge, Mary, upheld the suspension in her initial order.

"Mr. Robinson sought reconsideration, but the commission denied his request on August 30, 2011. Mr. Robinson timely filed his petition for judicial review on October 5, 2011."

The document pertaining to the "Issues" stated in quote, "Mr. Robinson raised seven issues on appeal to wit: (1) the ALJ charged the commission with an incomplete and incorrect definition of preponderance of the evidence, (2) the commission failed to make a finding that the agency imposed discipline at the lowest appropriate step for Mr. Robinson's misconduct, (3) the commission failed to state their reasoning for its decision, (4) the ALJ caused reversible error in admitting inadmissible prior disciplinary actions into record, (5) the commission erroneously adopted a definition that any activity could be construed as political activity in violation of the department's general orders and the Little Hatch Act or, alternatively, the commission applied the Little Hatch Act to Mr. Robinson in violation of his right to free speech and association, (6) the commission upheld discipline that was imposed in retaliation for Mr. Robinson's charges of race discrimination, and (7) the commission failed to articulate any reason why Mr. Robinson's ten-day suspension was warranted."

Another document pertained to "Analysis." It said in quote, "The court finds little merit as to a number of the arguments raised by Mr. Robinson. First, the commission has discretion to adopt the initial order issued by the ALJ that states that the agency has discretion not to exercise any review. It was not incumbent upon the commission to state an independent reason for upholding the ALJ's decision. The argument that the commission failed to state its reasoning is dismissed.

"Second, the instruction given by Administrative Law Judge Thomas to commission on preponderance of the evidence was appropriate. Under the APA, evidence in contested cases is not strictly limited to that which is admissible in court under traditional rules, but administrative officers may also admit evidence 'if it is of the type commonly relied upon by reasonably prudent men in the conduct of their affairs.' The challenge to the standard of preponderance of the evidence argument is dismissed.

"And third, Mr. Robinson's allegation of retaliation for filling charges of race discrimination against the department was not addressed by the ALJ or the commission. Mr. Robinson's allegation implicitly asserts that the burden of proof is upon the department to prove that it did not unlawfully retaliate against him. Typically, the burden is upon the individual who alleges retaliation to demonstrate that the adverse employment action was causally related to the protected activity in which the individual engaged.

"Mr. Robinson's claims that his protected activity involved his filing two different EEOC complaints. He submitted copies of the two EEOC complaints, and the first page of a letter from the EEOC dated November 6, 2008, stated that Mr. Robinson's claim failed. Mr. Robinson described in his proposed 'Finding of Facts' submitted to the commission the relationship between his EEOC complaint and the discipline that he received.

"One letter in the record reflects that Captain Steven complained to Major Wayne about Mr. Robinson's newspaper announcement to run for sheriff and Mr. Robinson's reference to the department's racist environment.

"Captain Steven testified at the level V hearing that he was upset by Mr. Robinson's action since they had a good working relationship when they worked together as troopers and that he felt like Mr. Robinson had used the election to 'stick me in the back.'

"The Tennessee Court of Appeals has addressed the requirements for proving an employment discrimination claim, stating that the establishment of all the prima facie elements by the plaintiff shifts the burden of production to the defendant to articulate a legitimate nondiscriminatory business reason for the challenged employment action. If the defendant can do so, then the burden shifts again to the plaintiff to present some evidence that the defendant's reasons are pretextual.

"Mr. Robinson may have carried his burden in demonstrating a prima facie case. He failed to present evidence that the defendant's reasons for the disciplinary actions were pretextual. Accordingly, this argument fails.

"The last issues raised by Mr. Robinson involved procedural due process violations and the appropriateness of the discipline imposed. The court reviewed the administrative record in detail with procedural due process as the focus of its inquiry. Mr. Robinson represented himself in each stage of the grievance proceedings and at the hearing before the ALJ.

"At the level III hearing on February 5, 2010, Director Hogan advised Mr. Robinson that courtroom procedures did not apply and asked him to waive the reading of the rules, to which Mr. Robinson agreed.

"Next, Sergeant Russell read the charges against Mr. Robinson, which included an allegation that in May 2009, June 2009, and early July 2009, he was in uniform when he ordered six magnetic campaign banners, traveled in his patrol car on duty to pick up the signs, and paid for the banners.

"Further, Sergeant Russell charged that on November 2, 2009, Mr. Robinson picked up and paid for two other banners while using his patrol car on duty and in uniform and that two years prior, on October 9, 2007, Mr. Robinson, in uniform, asked an individual for his support in the sheriff's election. Mr. Robinson asked to see the complaint filed against him, stating that he had not seen a complaint.

"Despite his repeated request to see the complaint filed against him, Mr. Robinson was required to answer questions before he could see his personnel file or the complaint.

"Mr. Robinson confirmed that as to the fourth allegation, he purchased campaign signs while in uniform. Mr. Robinson again asked to see the complaint against him, but a copy of it could not be found. Instead, an observer, Major Wayne, volunteered that the shop owners had contacted Captain Steven about Mr. Robinson's failure to pay for his banners.

"Mr. Robinson asked if the complaint had been filed against him for not paying a bill. Director Hogan told him that the owner only called to find out how to collect payment for the signs.

"Mr. Robinson then asked if the complaint was based upon his failure to pay on time and further inquired why his immediate supervisor had not notified him of the complaint and given him an opportunity to rectify the problem.

"Mr. Robinson was eventually advised at the hearing that the complaint was not about his failure to pay for his signs or a failure to pay on time but about campaign activity.

"In a written statement given to the Sergeant Officer on November 30, 2009, Mr. Robinson stated that he did not realize that he had done anything wrong because he wasn't in his county when he inquired about the cost of signs and when he purchased the signs. He wrote that he thought by giving his wife the signs, he would not be violating the general orders since he wasn't in his county. He wrote, 'I assure you, if given another chance and opportunity, I would never do this again. I really didn't realize the mess that it has caused. I felt pressured in paying Wentzel for the signs since I had owed them for quite some time.

"'Again, I should have waited. If I had to do it all over again, I would have had my wife to pay for and pick up the signs by herself. The problem was I didn't want her to get involved. If it hadn't been for a dream that I had, I wouldn't had her to come, and as I am thinking about it, I wish I hadn't.'

"When Mr. Robinson asked during the hearing why he was not contacted when the complaint was first made to give him an opportunity to rectify the problem, his question went unanswered. Under the circumstances, his request warrants review.

"During the level III hearing, Director Hogan denied that Mr. Robinson's nonpayment was an issue, stating that the merchant's phone call initiated the complaint. The whole thing, it doesn't matter how the department comes about knowing about a policy and/ or procedure violation. If it comes to knowledge, it goes through an inquiry or an investigation, whichever OPR chose to do.

"How the department acquired knowledge of a violation may not be critical. It is important, however, that Mr. Robinson be given procedural due process. Once the department knew that a violation had occurred, then the investigator officer's report of his conversation with Wentzel should have been sufficient to trigger the complaint.

"Instead, after Wentzel called and notified the department on November 1, 2010, that Mr. Robinson would be coming the next day, the sergeant officer hid near the sign shop to photograph Mr. Robinson in uniform when he arrived to pick up his signs rather than notifying Mr. Robinson that he had violated the act and providing him with notice at a meaningful time and in a meaningful manner. This conduct offends due process.

"Due process is flexible and calls for such procedural protections as the particular situation demands. Notice and opportunity for a hearing appropriate to the nature of the cause must precede the deprivation of life, liberty, or property. The nature of this case raises questions about the due process afforded to Mr. Robinson.

"Within an hour after Mr. Robinson was photographed on November 2, 2009, Sergeant Ray conducted a random line inspection of Mr. Robinson's patrol car. Nothing came of this inspection.

"Mr. Robinson immediately notified his supervisor, Sergeant Logan, and Lieutenant Hunter about the inspection and asked if they knew anything about the inspection. Both denied knowledge of the events occurring on November 2, 2009. At the level III hearing, Mr. Robinson learned that both Lieutenant Hunter and Logan knew of the events on November 2, 2009, before he spoke to them.

"Director Hogan stated that Mr. Robinson had been charged with violating departmental policy and that Mr. Robinson acknowledged that he knew about the Hatch Act and that Mr. Robinson knew he was not to campaign in any form or fashion while on duty in a patrol car.

"Mr. Robinson questioned how he had been campaigning because he had not displayed material in a state-owned building or his patrol car.

"Director Hogan stated that Mr. Robinson was using his patrol car for personal business and that Mr. Robinson had admitted as much. Mr. Robinson responded that the violation of general orders and the Hatch Act prohibited public officers from displaying public material in state-owned and/or controlled buildings or participating in political activity while on duty.

"Mr. Robinson stated that the only act he had done was to purchase some signs one time while on duty and that he gave the signs to his wife.

"The defendants, in its brief, states that the Little Hatch Act seeks in part to prohibit the inappropriate use of state employees and property for political purpose.

"The defendants cite the statute that prohibits state employees from performing political duties or functions not directly a part of their employment during the hours when they are required to be conducting the business of the state. The defendants, however, did not discuss the purpose of that statute.

"The intent of the mini-Hatch Act is 'to prohibit any political intimidations or coercion of any public officer or employee.' Under the act, state employees are not to interfere with an election or nomination directly or indirectly, solicit contributions for political purposes, promise benefits for political activity, deprive or threaten to deprive a person's employment, or use state-owned property for campaign advertising or activity.

"However, the defendants failed to quote the next section, which states as follows: 'Elected officials, state employees on leave or during those hours not required by law or administrative regulations to be conducting the business of the state, and persons duly qualified as candidates for public office are expressly excluded from the provisions of this section.'

"The defendants granted Mr. Robinson permission to run in a nonpartisan race for sheriff in his home county and to become a duly qualified candidate for public office. In this capacity, Mr. Robinson was excluded from the provisions of the very section cited by the defendants.

"Nonetheless, the department argues that its General Order 264, pursuant to the Little Hatch Act, prohibits its employees from 'participating in any political activity while on duty.'

"However, that argument is eviscerated by the Little Hatch Act, which states, 'No rule or regulation that has been promulgated or shall be promulgated by any department, division, agency, or bureau of the state government shall be more restrictive of the political activity of state employees on leave or during those hours not required by the law or administrative regulation to be conducting the business of the state than those restrictions already set forth in this section.'

"The department's general order is more restrictive than the act. Furthermore, the act exempted Mr. Robinson, as a duly qualified candidate, from its provisions. Accordingly, Mr. Robinson was not in violation of the general order or the Little Hatch Act.

"At the level IV hearing on March 17, 2010, Captain Brown conducted the hearing, and Sergeant Johnson read the same charges, adding that Mr. Robinson admitted purchasing campaign signs and transporting them in his patrol car while on duty, although Mr. Robinson denied that he had violated the Little Hatch Act.

"Sergeant Johnson again included the charge that Mr. Robinson engaged in political activity despite receiving two warning letters dated April 3, 2006, and August 8, 2007, which stated that the Little Hatch Act prohibited him from any political activity while on duty.

"Mr. Robinson denied ordering the signs while on duty but stated that on one occasion, he paid for the signs while he was in a marked patrol on duty. On March 18, 2010, Captain Brown concurred with the original disciplinary recommendation.

"Mr. Robinson questioned the introduction of the photographs taken of him at the Wentzel's store since he had not seen them. After examining the photos, Mr. Robinson tried to ask the witness if he had displayed campaign signs or banners on his patrol car, an act prohibited by the Little Hatch Act.

"When he attempted to ask the witness where the photos of his two campaign signs were taken and to clarify that location of the signs in the photos and said those two signs had nothing to do with him, the ALJ interrupted his questioning of the witness a number of times:

MR. ROBINSON: Where did you get these two campaign banners?

SERGEANT OFFICER: Got them from the owner of the sign shop.

MR. ROBINSON: Did you get those two campaign banners from me?

SERGEANT OFFICER: No.

MR. ROBINSON: Then did you introduce this picture and these two banners as evidence in your reports?

SERGEANT OFFICER: I don't think so.

MR. ROBINSON: Then if these campaign signs had nothing to do with me and they were inside of the building, why did you include these two banners in your investigative report of me having campaign banners in my possession?

THE COURT: Is that not your signs?

MR. ROBINSON: He said that he saw those signs in my possession.

THE COURT: So your question is that it had nothing to do with you. Your face is on the sign.

MR. ROBINSON: True enough.

THE COURT: Clearly, it has something to do with you.

MR. ROBINSON: True enough, but these two pictures that he had, these two banners right here, I had nothing to do with. They were inside of a building. He said he observed me having campaign signs in my possession when I came out of the building.

THE COURT: Okay. Rephrase your question because you need to ask a question that has a purpose and a point. But when your name is on the sign and your face is on one side of the signs, it is a bit absurd. So ask him why he had the pictures or ask him what he did with the pictures. But if you can't admit these have something to do with you, it's going to be a very long day.

MR. ROBINSON: You said you observed campaign banners in my possession, is that true?

SERGEANT OFFICER: Yes.

THE COURT: Is it true that you said it or is it true you saw it?

SERGEANT OFFICER: I saw—

THE COURT: Or both?

SERGEANT OFFICER: I saw campaign banners in his possession. I did not say they were these particular ones.

MR. ROBINSON: But you did not take pictures of me coming out of the sign shop with any signs?

SERGEANT OFFICER: The reason why there was not any pictures—

MR. ROBINSON: Don't you know?

THE COURT: I want to know the truth here. Go ahead and answer the question.

SERGEANT OFFICER: When you're taking pictures you—

THE COURT: Did you actually see him carrying campaign signs out of the Wentzel Sign Shop?

SERGEANT OFFICER: Yes."

Having that being said, it was obvious to John that the department's investigating officer was not telling the truth, and when his captain admitted while under oath that the department didn't have a policy after saying that there was a policy, John had come to the conclusion that the truth just wasn't in them.

Having that being said, John continued reading the court's documents.

The court continued and said, "Based upon the record, the department defined all political activity as anything that Mr. Robinson did as a candidate, including buying signs on duty and putting them in his patrol car, since it involved his campaign.

"When Mr. Robinson asked the witness if buying campaign signs and putting them in his car was campaigning on duty, Captain Steven said, 'Political activity, not necessarily on duty. That act will, in itself, benefit your campaign so that by doing so is campaign activity.'

"Mr. Robinson asked Captain Steven to confirm that the general order did not apply to signs inside his vehicle and only used the term 'displaying political materials.'

"After Captain Steven read the applicable section of the general order, Mr. Robinson again asked if the witness would define the term 'displaying.' Upon an objection by Ms. Martin, the department's attorney, the ALJ ruled that the question had been asked and answered.

"The ALJ interrupted Mr. Robinson to ask the witness whether the purchase of political campaign signs and putting them into a state trooper vehicle while on duty was political activity. Captain Steven stated that he believed so: 'If you purchase them on duty, I think that's in itself is a violation of the general order.'

"Another witness for the department, Sergeant Johnson, declared that Mr. Robinson was running for sheriff, and 'the mere fact that he still participated in political activity, that conduct is just not becoming of a state trooper.' Sergeant Johnson charged Mr. Robinson with conduct unbecoming an employee of the state service because Mr. Robinson had been reminded of the Little Hatch Act and the department and 'he still participated in political activity.' Sergeant Johnson testified that buying political banners in uniform in a patrol car was clear-cut political activity, 'things done to further his chances or further his' to gain support for his campaign, and he did so while on duty.

"The ALJ stated that participating in political activity while on duty was not approved by the department and violated the general orders, state law, and the department's rules. She stated that buying campaign signs while on duty is political activity because it is part of running one's political campaign. She found that transporting campaign signs was political activity. Accordingly, she found that Mr. Robinson had participated in political activity while on duty in violation of the department's general orders, state law, and the department's rules. She made no analysis of the discipline imposed upon Mr. Robinson, merely concluding that ten days without pay was appropriate.

"The actions of the ALJ during the hearing as cited above reflect a lack of neutrality, which may have undermind Mr. Robinson's due process rights to a full and fair hearing. She made general reference to the rules, general orders, and statutes but failed to analyze the Little Hatch Act and the exemption afforded to Mr. Robinson as set out above.

"The department granted Mr. Robinson's request to run for a nonpartisan office. He was not required to leave his position although he was transferred to work in another county from the one of which he qualified to run for office.

"Mr. Robinson's questioning during the various hearings reflects that he had closely read the same statutes. He did not display his campaign materials on his patrol car. The department used a much broader definition of campaign activity remotely connected to Mr. Robinson's campaign, including preparations such as buying signs or banners, even though these were not displayed.

"The Little Hatch Act specifically excluded qualified candidates for public office from the provisions of the act, with the exception of interfering with an election or a nomination.

"Mr. Robinson was a duly qualified candidate for public office, and his conduct was excluded from the Little Hatch Act and, correspondingly, the department's general orders and rules.

"Nevertheless, the commission's final order adopted the ALJ's initial order.

"As explained above, the final order was arbitrary and capricious, in excess of statutory authority, violating the specific exclusion afforded to Mr. Robinson under the very same statute that the department relied upon, was made in an improper manner, and was unsupported by substantial and material evidence.

"The final order of the commission upholding the decision of the ALJ is reversed, and the ten-day suspension without pay is set aside. Costs are assessed against the department.

"It is so ordered."

Having that being said, John filed a lawsuit against the department. As a result thereof, he was ordered not to discuss the results.

Having that being said, as a result of the Information Act, anyone that would be interested in the results could obtain the final outcome.

As fate would have it, John took a stand. He finally obtained closure. His case was was put on line for all to see.

SWEENEY v. TENNESSEE DEPARTMENT OF SAFETY

No. 1:12-0112.

LUIS EASTMAN SWEENEY, Plaintiff, v. TENNESSEE DEPARTMENT OF SAFETY, et al., Defendants.
United States District Court, M.D. Tennessee, Columbia Division.
June 8, 2015.

Attorney(s) appearing for the Case

Luis Eastman Sweeney, Plaintiff, represented by <u>Andrew B. Love</u>, Law Office of Andrew Love.

Tennessee Department of Safety, An Agency of the State of Tennessee, Defendant, represented by <u>John W. Dalton</u>, Tennessee Attorney General's Office.

Bill Gibbons, Commissioner, Tennessee Department of Safety, Defendant, represented by <u>John W. Dalton</u>, Tennessee Attorney General's Office.

State of Tennessee, Defendant, represented by <u>John W. Dalton</u>, Tennessee Attorney General's Office.

Bill Haslam, Governor of the State of Tennessee, Defendant, represented by <u>John W. Dalton</u>, Tennessee Attorney General's Office.

REPORT AND RECOMMENDATION

JOHN S. BRYANT, *Magistrate Judge.*

TO: THE HONORABLE TODD J. CAMPBELL

Pending in this case is Defendants' motion summary judgment (Docket Entry No. 50), to which Plaintiff has responded in opposition (Docket Entry No. 55). Defendants have filed a reply (Docket Entry No. 63).

For the reasons stated below, the undersigned Magistrate Judge finds that there are genuine disputes regarding material facts, and that Defendants' motion for summary judgment therefore should be denied.

STATEMENT OF THE CASE

Plaintiff Luis Sweeney is a retired Tennessee State Trooper who has filed this action pursuant to Title VII of the Civil Rights Act of 1964 alleging racial discrimination and retaliation by his former employer, the Tennessee Department of Safety (Docket Entry No. 45). Also named as Defendants are Bill Gibbons, Commissioner of the Tennessee Department of Safety, and Governor Bill Haslam, who are sued in their official capacities.

Defendants have filed an answer denying liability (Docket Entry No. 46) and they have now filed their motion for summary judgment.

STANDARD OF REVIEW

A party may obtain summary judgment by showing "that there is no genuine dispute as to any material fact and that the movant is entitled to judgment as a matter of law. *See* Fed. R. Civ. P. 56(a); *Covington v. Knox County School Sys.*, 205 F.3d 912, 914 (6th Cir. 2000). The moving party bears the initial burden of satisfying the court that the standards of Rule 56 have been met. *See Martin v. Kelley*, 803 F.2d 236, 239 n.4 (th Cir. 1986). The ultimate question to be addressed is whether there exists any genuine dispute of material fact. *See Anderson v. Liberty Lobby, Inc.*, 477 U.S. 242, 248 (1986); *Covington*, 205 F.3d at 914 (citing *Celotex Corp. v. Catrett*, 477 U.S. 317, 325 (1986)). If so, summary judgment is inappropriate.

To defeat a properly supported motion for summary judgment, the nonmoving party must set forth specific facts showing that there is a genuine issue of material fact for trial. If the party does not so respond, summary judgment will be entered if appropriate. Fed. R. Civ. P. 56(e). The nonmoving party's burden of providing specific facts demonstrating that there remains a genuine issue of material fact for trial is triggered once the moving party shows an absence of evidence to support the nonmoving party's case. *Celotex,* 477 U.S. at 325. A genuine issue of material fact exists "if the evidence is such that a reasonable jury could return a verdict for the nonmoving party." *Anderson,* 477 U.S. at 248. In ruling on a motion for summary judgment, the Court must construe the evidence in the light most favorable to the nonmoving party, drawing all justifiable inferences in its favor. *See Matsushita Elec. Indus. Co. v. Zenith Radio Corp.,* 475 U.S. 574, 587 (1986).

STATEMENT OF UNDISPUTED FACTS

The following facts appear to be undisputed in the record:

Plaintiff Sweeney was employed for 25 years as a State Trooper by the Tennessee Department of Safety. At all pertinent times, Sweeney's home county was Maury County. Sweeney is an African-American, and for much of his employment he was the only African-American Trooper in his district.

Sweeney ran for elected office as Sheriff of Maury County in 2010. As required by department policies, Sweeney sought permission from his superiors to run for this office. The department granted permission for Sweeney to seek the office of Sheriff, but informed him that if he did run for this office he would be temporarily assigned to work in an adjoining county during his campaign. On the day after Sweeney publicly announced his candidacy for the office of Sheriff of Maury County, he was temporarily reassigned to Marshall County for a period of approximately 19 months until shortly after the election in 2010. Sweeney alleges that this temporary reassignment to an adjoining county during the pendency of his campaign for office was racially motivated because white Troopers who ran for elected office were not similarly reassigned.

Sweeney filed charges of racial discrimination against the Department of Safety on May 16, 2008, December 31, 2008, and on May 26, 2009 (Docket Entry No. 45-2). Each of these charges allege racial discrimination by the Department of Safety based upon the temporary reassignment of Sweeney to Marshall County during his campaign for Sheriff of Maury County.

In November 2009, Sweeney became the subject of an internal investigation by the Department of Safety based upon a claim that he had violated state law and Department policy by engaging in political activities while on duty as a State Trooper. This investigation led to Sweeney being disciplined with a 10-day suspension without pay in January 2010.

Sweeney appealed his disciplinary suspension through all levels of appeal within the Department of Safety, and the suspension was affirmed at every administrative level. Sweeney then appealed his suspension to the Chancery Court of Davidson County pursuant to the Tennessee Uniform Administrative Procedures Act, Tenn. Code Ann. § 4-5-322. The Court found that the Department's suspension of Sweeney was "arbitrary and capricious, in excess of statutory authority, violated the exclusion afforded Mr. Sweeney under the very statute that the Department relied upon, and was made in an improper manner and was unsupported by substantial and material evidence." (Docket Entry No. 60-5 at 21). Sweeney alleges that this internal investigation that led to his suspension was instigated in retaliation for his engaging in protected activity, the filing of the charges of discrimination with the EEOC.

ANALYSIS

Discrimination Claim Based Upon Reassignment to Marshall County. Title VII prohibits employment discrimination based upon the employee's race. 42 U.S.C. § 2000e-2(a)(1). Sweeney claims that he was reassigned to Marshall County during his campaign for Sheriff of Maury County because of his race in violation of Title VII. Sweeney has offered no direct evidence of discrimination. Employment discrimination cases based upon circumstantial evidence are analyzed under the three-step framework announced in *McDonnell Douglas Corp. v. Green,* 411 U.S. 792 (1973). The employee must first demonstrate a *prima facie* case of race discrimination; the burden then shifts to the employer to offer a legitimate, nondiscriminatory reason for its actions; finally, the burden shifts back to the employee to show that the employer's professed reason is a pretext for discrimination. *Chattman v. Toho Tenax America, Inc.,* 686 F.3d 339, 347 (6th Cir. 2012).

In order to demonstrate a *prima facie* case of discrimination under Title VII, Sweeney must establish (1) that he is a member of a protected class; (2) that he suffered an adverse employment action; (3) that he was qualified for the position; and (4) that a similarly situated employee outside the protected class was treated more favorably than he was. *Dodd v. Donahoe,* 715 F.3d 151, 156 (6th Cir. 2013). From the record in this case, the undersigned Magistrate Judge finds that Sweeney has offered evidence to support each of these four claims. First, Sweeney as an African-American is a member of a protected class. Second, he was transferred from his home county to an adjoining county for duty while he ran for the office of Sheriff. Although the parties dispute whether this temporary reassignment amounted to a materially adverse employment action, the undersigned finds that this temporary transfer could be found to amount to an adverse action against Sweeney. Third, Sweeney was clearly qualified for the position he filled, since he satisfactorily performed his duties as a State Trooper for a number of years. Finally, Sweeney testified in his affidavit and in his deposition that at least some white Troopers who ran for elective office were not reassigned to adjoining counties (Docket Entry No. 60-7 at 27-28 and Docket Entry No. 59 at 2).

Defendants state that Sweeney was reassigned temporarily to Marshall County during his campaign for Sheriff of Maury County in compliance with department policy designed to minimize claims that State Troopers and the Department of Safety were improperly using their offices or positions in local political campaigns. Michael Walker testified in deposition that he was made Colonel of the Tennessee Highway Patrol on March 1, 2006. He testified that in the months before that date the Highway Patrol had come under intense scrutiny and criticism in the public media based on claims of cronyism and political influence in hiring and promotions, and that in response the agency had undergone a dramatic change in top leadership. The new leaders, including Walker, had been charged with eliminating politics and restoring professionalism within Highway Patrol (Docket Entry

No. 60-9 at 3-4). Walker further testified that after he became colonel in March 2006, the Highway Patrol adopted a policy of assigning Troopers who ran for elected office in their home county to work temporarily in an adjoining county during their campaign for office. According to Walker, this policy was adopted "to remove some of that stigma that we had with the political involvement." (Docket Entry No. 60-9 at 4).

Tracy Trott testified that he became Lieutenant Colonel in the Highway Patrol in 2006. He testified that, to his memory, everyone in the Highway Patrol who ran for elected office since 2006 had been moved to another country during the period of the campaign (Docket Entry No. 54-1 at 8). Trott explained that this policy was implemented in order to protect the best interests of the Department of Safety and the Trooper to avoid potential criticism by the Trooper's political opponent that the Trooper was performing political activities while on duty or otherwise using his official position improperly to gain political advantage. (*Id.*)

The evidence further shows that the Department of Safety on May 15, 2006, adopted a General Order entitled "Political Activities." (Docket Entry No. 60-3). This general order contains certain procedural guidelines for employees seeking elected positions, including the employee's obligation to notify his immediate supervisor by written memorandum of his intention to run in any political race. Following a review by the Commissioner's Office, the employee was to be notified in writing of the approval or disapproval of the employee's intention to run for office. Significantly, this general order fails to contain any mention of a temporary reassignment of an employee to another county for the duration of the employee's political campaign. On December 1, 2013, the Tennessee Department of Safety and Homeland Security adopted a general order dealing with "political activity," which apparently was intended to supersede earlier versions (Docket Entry No. 60-4). This general order does contain a provision stating that the Commissioner or Colonel, "for the good of the service," may change an employee's work assignment to avoid potential conflicts during the campaign and election process (*Id.* at 4).

The undersigned Magistrate Judge, upon review of the evidence, finds that there is a genuine issue of material facts regarding when the Department of Safety adopted a consistent, unvarying policy of temporarily assigning a State Trooper to an adjoining county while such Trooper was engaged in a campaign for elected office. The testimony of Mike Walker and Tracy Trott, referenced above, seems to state that such policy was adopted in the spring of 2006. However, the general order on political activities dated May 15, 2006, fails to contain a statement of such policy. Moreover, insofar as the record indicates, a written policy of such temporary reassignment did not appear in a general order until December 1, 2013. This inconsistency, coupled with the testimony of Plaintiff Sweeney that other Troopers who ran for elective office were not reassigned to a different county, creates a genuine issue of material fact, and suggests the possibility that Defendants' stated reason for reassigning Sweeney to Marshall County was pretextual. Given this uncertainty in the record, the undersigned Magistrate Judge cannot find that the undisputed proof establishes the absence of a genuine dispute of material fact for trial.

Retaliation Based Upon the Internal Investigation. Sweeney claims that the Department of Safety instigated an internal investigation that resulted in a 10-day suspension from work without pay in retaliation for his prior charges of discrimination to the EEOC. To establish a *prima facie* case of retaliation under Title VII, an employee must show (1) that he engaged in activity protected by Title VII; (2) that his exercise of such protected activity was known by the Defendant employer; (3) that the employer thereafter took an action that was materially adverse to the employee; and (4) that a causal connection existed between the protected activity and the materially adverse action. *Laster v. City of Kalamazoo,* 746 F.3d 714, 730 (6th Cir. 2014). Moreover, a Title VII retaliation claim must be proved to traditional principles of but-for causation, which "requires proof that the unlawful retaliation would not have occurred in the absence of the alleged wrongful action or actions of the employer." *Id.* at 731 (citing *Univ. of Texas Southwest Med. Ctr v. Nassar,* 133 S.Ct. 2517, 2533 (2013)).

If the plaintiff employee establishes a *prima facie* case of retaliation, the burden shifts to the employer to articulate a legitimate, non-discriminatory reason for the employment action. If the employer does so, the burden shifts back to the plaintiff employee to offer competent evidence of pretext. *Chattman,* 686 F.3d at 349.

Here, Sweeney had filed three charges of racial discrimination against the Department of Safety before the institution of the internal investigation in November 2009. In addition, it is undisputed that the Department was aware of Sweeney's charges. It is further undisputed that the Department commenced an internal affairs investigation of Sweeney that resulted in a disciplinary suspension for his engaging in political activities while on duty. Finally, Sweeney has established that on January 6, 2009, Captain Steven Hazard, Sweeney's superior, wrote a letter to Major Wayne Skinner complaining about Sweeney's charges of discrimination filed with the EEOC as well as apparent statements by Sweeney to the local newspaper, including accusations of racist behavior by the Department (Docket Entry No. 60-10). From the foregoing, the undersigned finds that Plaintiff Sweeney has offered sufficient evidence to demonstrate a *prima facie* case of retaliation under Title VII.

Defendants assert that the internal investigation of Sweeney was prompted not by racial retaliation against Sweeney but by an unsolicited inquiry from a local merchant that suggested Sweeney was engaging in political activity while on duty as a State Trooper. Specifically, the merchant asserted that Sweeney was scheduled to come to her business in order to pick up campaign signs for his Sheriff campaign while on duty. The Department dispatched an officer to obtain pictures of Sweeney picking up these campaign signs while wearing his uniform and driving a State Trooper patrol car.

As referenced above, the Chancery Court which eventually heard Sweeney's appeal of his disciplinary suspension found that the Department's investigation of Sweeney violated Sweeney's right to procedural due process and that the disciplinary suspension awarded against Sweeney "was arbitrary and capricious, in excess of statutory authority, violated the specific exclusion afforded Mr. Sweeney under the very statute that the Department relied upon, and was made in an improper manner and was unsupported by substantial and material evidence." (Docket Entry No. 60-5 at 21). While the ruling of the Chancery Court is not wholly dispositive of the issue of pretext in this action, the undersigned finds that it at least creates a genuine dispute regarding the reason that the Department instituted an internal affairs investigation against Sweeney.

In summary, the undersigned Magistrate Judge finds that the record before the Court fails to establish the absence of any genuine dispute of material fact for trial. On the contrary, the undersigned finds that there are material factual issues in this case with respect to Sweeney's racial discrimination claim as well as his retaliation claim that should be decided by a jury. The undersigned therefore finds that the Defendants' motion for summary judgment should be denied.

RECOMMENDATION

For the reasons stated above, the undersigned Magistrate Judge finds that Defendants' motion for summary judgment (Docket Entry No. 50) should be denied.

Under Rule 72(b) of the Federal Rules of Civil Procedure, any party has 14 days from receipt of this Report and Recommendation in which to file any written objections to this Recommendation with the District Court. Any party opposing said objections shall have 14 days from receipt of any objections filed in this Report in which to file any responses to said objections. Failure to file specific objections within 14 days of receipt of this Report and Recommendation can constitute a waiver of further appeal of this Recommendation. *Thomas v. Arn,* 474 U.S. 140, 106 S.Ct. 466, 88 L.Ed.2d 435 (1985), *Reh'g denied,* 474 U.S.

About the Author

I am married and I have two adult children and several grandkids.

I was born and raised within a military environment. I believed I was groomed to serve, not as a slave but as a man who cares about humanity.

I had always wanted to be in a position of power and to have authority. I chose to become a law enforcement officer so that who ever would come in contact with me would know that one would be treated fair and justly and the color of ones skin wouldn't be a factor in the way I would enforce the law.

I began my law enforcement career by serving my country as a military policeman during the Viet Nam War and as a combat military policeman in the Army National Guard. I was also a deputy sheriff when I had attended college. I had earned a B.S. degree in Criminal Justice and an A.S. degree in Audio Production.

I served my state at a juvenile correctional institution and as a state trooper. I became the first black trooper to retire in the district of my residence.

I have written two other books titled, "The System of Things I and II."

9 781649 521972